Jungle Hearts of Costa Rica

Jungle Hearts of Costa Rica

Answering the Call to Rescue

Mike Graeber

Forward by Michael Henning

Editorial Development
Mike Graeber and Michael Henning

Jungle Hearts Publishing

First edition.

Editorial Development by
Mike Graeber and Michael Henning

Foreword by Michael Henning

Published by
Jungle Hearts Publishing

ISBN: 979-8-9954420-0-4

Cover photograph and interior photographs courtesy of Mike Graeber unless otherwise noted.

This is a work of nonfiction. Some names or identifying details may have been changed to protect the privacy of individuals.

Printed in the United States of America

For Jerry

Dedicated to those who don't have a voice.....

And those who choose to speak for them

You don't need a big plan to make a big difference.
___Mike Graeber

Foreword

Mike Graeber had recently returned from Costa Rica after spending more than twenty years living among the wildlife and helping build animal sanctuaries in the rainforest. Mike and I and several of our high school wrestling teammates had gathered in Denver Colorado to see our old teammate Bob Sisler get inducted into the National Wrestling Hall of Fame and we were enjoying a reunion at Bob and Ginger's house afterwards.

Someone asked Mike about his time in Costa Rica, and he began to describe a moment when he was attacked by a Geoffroy's spider monkey. As Mike vividly described how the encounter unfolded, you could feel the danger, the tension, the chaos, and the unpredictability of working with wild animals. It all came alive.

It was one of those moments where everyone in the room could picture the scene in their minds clearly.

And that was when it struck me: these weren't just stories to share among friends. They were stories that needed to be written down. Mike also knew he had lived an extraordinary chapter of life there, but like many people who have experienced something unusual, he wasn't quite sure how to turn those experiences into a book or how such a story could ever be published. We both knew this had to be a book.

One of the most remarkable things about Mike's story is that he is not a veterinarian or a trained biologist. By trade, he is a construction worker. But from the time he was a child, when he once nursed an injured blue jay back to health, he carried a deep instinct to protect and care for animals.

Years later that instinct took him to Costa Rica, a place very different from the life he had known. There, through persistence, compassion, and determination, he helped rescue animals and build sanctuaries that gave many of them a second chance.

The title Jungle Hearts could not be more appropriate.

Anyone who has rescued animals knows the experience can bring a kind of joy that is difficult to describe. But it can also bring heartbreak. Many of the animals Mike worked with would be described by most people simply as "wild animals." To him, they often became something much more personal—members of an extended family.

Just like the dog or cat waiting for you at home, these animals formed bonds with the person who cared for them. They trusted him. They depended on him. And in many cases, their hearts were just as capable of breaking as any human's when those bonds were separated.

What you are about to read is a glimpse into those years in the jungle—years filled with danger, humor, compassion, and the extraordinary connections that can form between humans and the creatures who share this planet with us.

— Mike Henning

Table of Contents

Prologue - A New Beginning xvi

Chapter 1 - The Road to Lagunas del Barú 1

Chapter 2 - The Banana Bread Table 5

Chapter 3 - The Banana Bread Table Takes Off 9

Chapter 4 - Heckle and Jeckle 11

Chapter 5 - Bubba 15

Chapter 6 - Bubba Meets Jerry and Tony..............................17

Chapter 7 - Bubba Meets Hollywood 21

Chapter 8 - Jerry 25

Chapter 9 - The Bridge at 1:00 AM 27

Chapter 10 - D.A.W.G. 31

Chapter 11 - A Golden Opportunity 35

Chapter 12 - The Sorcerer of Violin Island............................39

Chapter 13 - The Call That Changed Everything....................45

Chapter 14 - Osa Santuario de Animales 49

Chapter 15 - The First Arrivals 55

Chapter 16 - Tubby the Tipisquenti 59

Chapter 17 - Population Explosion 63

Chapter 18 - Chester and Festus 69

Chapter 19 - Gomer the Tamandua..75

Chapter 20 - Trouble in Paradise 79

Chapter 21 - Plan B... Activated! 83

Chapter 22 - Alturas Wildlife Sanctuary is Born.................... 87

Chapter 23 - Construction and Conflict 93

Chapter 24 - Moving Day 1 97

Chapter 25 - Moving Day 2 103

Contents (continued)

Chapter 26 - Getting Ready to Open 105

Chapter 27 - The First Tours Begin 109

Chapter 28 - New Arrivals 113

Chapter 29 - More New Arrivals/Trouble in Paradise..........117

Chapter 30 - Escapes and Losses 121

Chapter 31 - New Problems, New Opportunities 127

Chapter 32 - New Horizons and New Challenges 133

Chapter 33 - New Beginnings..139

Chapter 34 - Arrival in the Cloud Forest..............................143

Chapter 35 - Much to Do 147

Chapter 36 - The Great Parrot Release..................................153

Chapter 37 - The Return of Bubba and Blossom...................159

Chapter 38 - New Arrivals and New Beginnings...................165

Chapter 39 - Construction and a Fat Raccoon 171

Chapter 40 - The Garden Opens..175

Chapter 41 - Tommy Comes Home..179

Chapter 42 - Bubba's Big Leap..183

Chapter 43 - Saved by a Forked Stick....................................187

Chapter 44 - Reflection in the Cloud Forest..........................193

Epilogue 197

About the Author..199

Prologue -A New Beginning

By Mike Graeber

In 1997, after many years of hard work, I decided it was finally time to take a real vacation. I chose Costa Rica. Friends had told me for years what a paradise it was—lush, peaceful, full of life.

I went down with an open mind and an open heart, just to see it for myself. What I found was exactly what they'd said: a breathtaking country, warm and welcoming people, and a financial system where my money could stretch a whole lot further than back home.

When I returned to the U.S., I couldn't shake the feeling that something had shifted. I started what I called my "three-year move-to-Costa-Rica plan." By October 2000, that plan had come to life. I sold my company, my house, and most of what I owned. I loaded up my two dogs and my cat into a rental car and drove to the airport in Tampa.

Two days later, we landed in Costa Rica. I still remember standing outside that little house I'd bought—a simple place tucked into the side of a mountain. The air was warm and heavy with the scent of jungle flowers. Birds I'd never seen before called out across the valley. From the porch, I could look out over the Pacific Ocean, endless and blue

It was quiet. I was alone with my animals. And I knew I'd made the right choice.

That's where the real story begins.

What follows is a tale of animals, adventure, and the unforgettable characters I met over the next 20 years living and working in Costa Rica. Some of it is funny, some of it's wild, and it will stay with me—and maybe you—forever.

Chapter 1

The Road to Lagunas del Barú

The new life I'd dreamed about was finally beginning. It was October 30th when I packed up my two dogs, my cat, and the last scraps of my old life into a rental car and left Colorado behind. I was heading for the airport in Tampa, Florida, but in truth, I was heading for something much bigger: a wild, beautiful unknown.

A couple of days later, I touched down at Juan Sanataria International Airport in San José, Costa Rica. The air was warm, heavy with the scent of blooming tropical flowers and distant rain. Even the sounds were different, strange birds calling in the trees, and that low, ever-present hum of jungle life in the background.

I found a modest hotel near the city and got in touch with a cab driver I'd met on a previous trip. He greeted me with a wide smile and a hearty "Pura vida, amigo!" the kind of greeting that makes you feel like you belong, even if you don't yet.

The next day, around noon, we loaded my luggage and my very confused pets into the cab and began the long, winding journey to my new home in Lagunas del Barú, near the coastal town of Dominical. The drive took us through mountain passes where waterfalls spilled right onto the road, through small towns with roadside fruit stands selling ripe mangoes, guanábanas, and sweet pineapples, and along stretches of jungle so thick and green it looked like something from a movie.

Dominical is a little surf town perched on the edge of the Pacific, about halfway between Nicaragua and Panama. It's known as the entrance to Costa Rica's southern tropical zone, and rightly so. Here, the jungle doesn't politely stop at the edge of town. It pours down the mountains, spills onto the beaches, and grows wherever it pleases.That's exactly why I'd chosen it. I'd been here before and fallen in love with the place. So before I even sold my house in Colorado, I bought a small two-bedroom home on five acres of sloping land, high on a jungle-covered hillside. The elevation was around 600 feet, just high enough for ocean views and cool breezes at night.

The house sat about two and a half miles inland, tucked in the jungle above Dominical. The roads up there were steep and rocky, more goat path than highway. But the view made up for it: a sweeping panorama of the Pacific Ocean, surrounded by orchids, heliconias, and the sounds of parrots, toucans, and howler monkeys in the trees.

Dominical itself had a raw, unfinished charm. Back then, it had dirt roads, a single small grocery store, a few open-air restaurants with tin roofs, and just a couple of low-key surf hostels. But what it lacked in polish, it made up for with world-class waves and sunsets that could stop your heart.

As I began to settle in, I quickly realized that a car wasn't just a luxury, it was a necessity. The roads were unforgiving, and the nearest anything was always at the bottom of a long, bumpy descent. After asking around, I found a red Toyota truck for sale. The owner was an American who happened to be out of the country, but I managed to track him down and strike a deal.

With that, I had my first taste of jungle problem solving. And my first win. I had wheels.

The next challenge was electricity. I won't bore you with the details, but let's just say nothing happens quickly in rural Costa Rica. A few days, a few favors, and probably a few colones slipped to the right hands later, the lights finally came on. Now I could begin exploring.

On the second night in my new home, I figured it was probably okay to let the cat out. Whisper had always been an outdoor cat, and I figured she'd stay close and she did. For about twenty minutes. Then she came blasting back into the house like a little furry cannonball, every hair on her body standing straight up, snarling like a wildcat. I knew that look. Something had scared the living daylights out of her. I never saw what it was, but I had a good guess.

There's a creature here called a Zorro one of Costa Rica's marsupials. It's kind of like a possum, if a possum had sharper teeth and an attitude. These things move fast and aren't shy about picking a fight with anything smaller than a raccoon. Whisper, who had grown up stalking field mice in tidy suburban gardens, had never seen anything like it. Honestly, it was hilarious.

She stayed inside for a few days after that, keeping a wary eye on the jungle. But little by little, she adapted. Before long, she was slinking through the underbrush like she owned the place. She'd become a full-on jungle cat.

And just like that, we were home.

Chapter 2

The Banana Bread Table

When I first settled on the mountain in Lagunas, I leaned into what I knew best: concrete work. After more than two decades in the construction trade back in Denver, I figured I could make some money and help out neighbors by pouring patios, driveways, and steps. But Costa Rica had different plans. You can't just order a truckload of concrete in the jungle. Everything had to be mixed by hand one bag at a time, shoveled into a small mixer, then pushed in wheelbarrows by sweating, slipping laborers across uneven ground. It was exhausting, labor intensive, hot, and completely unsustainable. I started asking myself: What else can I do here that doesn't involve mixing concrete under a blazing sun? That's when banana bread changed everything.

Jerry was visiting, along with his daughter, and a friend of mine who happened to be a great baker had just whipped up a batch of fresh banana bread. Jerry's daughter took one bite and said, "You could sell this." I don't know what it was about the way she said it, but it landed. I looked around at where I was, a small surf town with no bakery, no real store, and a lot of surfers with the munchies. There was only one little restaurant in Dominical back then, Tortilla Flats, but nothing else. No snacks. No sweets. No easy food. Except bananas. There were bananas everywhere. And just like that, the idea hit me full force. I wasn't going to pour concrete, I was going to sell banana bread.

The First Day on the Beach

We baked up a dozen small loaves of banana bread, along with a few batches of chocolate chip and oatmeal raisin cookies. I loaded everything up and made my way down to the beach. Right across from Tortilla Flats, there was a sandy stretch dotted with old concrete picnic tables, huge, immovable slabs with built-in benches, just steps from the surf. I staked my claim on one. It was shaded by palms and perfectly positioned between the road and the water. I threw a tablecloth over it, tied up my hammock nearby between two trees, laid out my baked goods, and sat down. I wasn't just selling banana bread, I was selling banana bread from a hammock to surfers. And it worked.

I didn't know it then, but that was the beginning of the next eight years of my life. By the end of the first week, people were already calling me "Banana Bread Mike." For over a year, I was the first and only vendor on that beach, and the only gringo vendor anyone had ever seen there. Dominical was still quiet back then. Untouched. I broke the ice, and set the tone for what that beachfront would eventually become. Now that same stretch is packed from end to end with vendors. Booths and tables and trucks block the view of the ocean. From the road, you can't even see the water anymore. But back then I was it, just me, a table full of warm banana bread, and the waves rolling in. And it wasn't just about banana bread. That table became my headquarters. My hub. I met people from all over the world, actors, athletes, travelers, nomads, surfers, wanderers. I sold real estate from that table. I launched DAWG, a grassroots effort to spay and neuter beach dogs. I connected with people who would later help me start my first wildlife sanctuary. It was more than a business. It was a turning point. It was the first seed of everything that came next.

Author's Note

People ask me sometimes: how did you survive down there? I tell them I stopped trying to be who I was in Denver, and started listening to what the jungle wanted from me. The banana bread table wasn't just about income. It was about roots, planting myself in a place and seeing what could grow. And it grew more than I ever expected.

—Mike

Chapter 3

The Banana Bread Table Takes Off

When I first started selling banana bread, I didn't realize I was starting what would become the best job I ever had, and one of the best decisions of my life. Each morning, I'd head out early to the same beachside spot where I had taken over a large concrete table, under the shade of a sea almond tree. I'd lay out my loaves of banana bread, brewed with just the right balance of love, cinnamon, and tropical sweetness. Then I'd sling up my hammock nearby, grab a hot cup of coffee from across the street, and settle in.

That first month was pure magic. Every day, as the Pacific breeze swept over the beach and the palm fronds whispered above me, I'd watch the world come to me. Not just tourists in flip-flops or kids with surfboards—but people from every walk of life. Models. Movie stars. Professional athletes. Sitcom actors recognizable from American TV. Even politicians stopped by, drawn in by the smell of fresh-baked banana bread and the mellow atmosphere of the jungle-meets-beach setup. And of course, there were always girls in bikinis drifting past with the tide.

Over time, the Banana Bread Table became more than a place to sell snacks. It became a hub of conversation, of laughter, of community. And from that hub, a lot of great ideas were born. One of those ideas was D.A.W.G.—the Dominical Animal Welfare Group. I'd been watching the beach dogs, many of them hungry, mangy, and uncared for. I couldn't just sit there and ignore them. So I took action. DAWG was born to spay, neuter, and provide basic veterinary care to the beach dogs of Dominical. It wasn't long before we expanded to help as many dogs in the surrounding areas as we could reach. And it all started with one guy, one table, and a loaf of banana bread.

The Banana Bread Table also became the birthplace of my first animal sanctuary. It was around that time I realized this wasn't just a job anymore—it was a lifestyle with a purpose. The people I met, the causes I joined, the creatures I cared for… it was all deeply connected. Then came the beef jerky. At the time, jerky was practically unknown in Costa Rica. The locals, Ticos, would wrinkle their noses and ask, "Why are you selling black meat?" But all it took was one taste. Suddenly, they couldn't get enough. People were buying in bulk. Word spread. There were nights I'd wake up to knocking on my front door, locals in need of a jerky fix. They weren't shy about it either. One guy said, "Señor Mike, my brother sent me from two towns over. He says you have the good stuff!" And I did.

For eight straight years, the Banana Bread Table was my center of gravity. It was where I showed up every day, except on the rare rainy days or when I had business up in town. But otherwise, I was there. And it was a joy. Today, if you walk the beach in Dominical, you'll see it packed shoulder to shoulder with vendors. But back then, I was the first, the only one, the lone gringo selling banana bread from a picnic table near the surf.

Chapter 4

Heckle and Jeckle

It started with a five gallon bucket. Three years into my life in Lagunas, a man called and said he had found two birds that needed help. He didn't want to explain over the phone. "Just meet me at the bottom of the hill," he said. When I arrived, he handed me a worn plastic bucket lined with grass. Nestled inside were two tiny, wide-eyed creatures, Chestnut-Mandible Toucans, just barely recognizable. Their feathers were patchy. Their eyes looked dazed. They had been blown out of their nest in a storm, found on the ground, half-covered in ants. They looked like they weren't long for this world. But they were alive. I brought them up the hill and got to work. I cleaned them up gently, feather by feather, beak by beak. I had learned from a local friend that toucans raised in captivity could survive on papaya and banana alone. But I'd seen enough of animal nutrition to know better, so I added scrambled egg to the mix. Protein for strength. I named them Heckle and Jeckle, not because I expected them to cause trouble, but because, with birds, you often get more than you bargained for.

For weeks, they stayed close. I hand-fed them, sheltered them, watched them grow. When they were strong enough, I opened their cage and let them live on a perch on the patio, where the wind was warm and the jungle light shifted through the leaves like watercolor.

They practiced flying from there, tentative flaps, soft landings, wild tumbles. And as they got better, they started to spend more time in the trees nearby. But they never strayed far. Whenever I came home, I'd whistle a certain note, always the same. Within seconds, I'd hear the squawk of recognition, and both birds would come flying toward me, wings outstretched like old friends rushing in for a hug. Jeckle would land neatly and wait for food. Heckle would slap me in the back of the head. That became his favorite game, sneak up from behind, hit me just hard enough to sting, then flap off in a burst of cackling joy. It was like being ambushed by a feathered prankster who thought he was a jungle ninja.

Jeckle, on the other hand, was more delicate in every way. He was smaller. His feathers were sparse. His flight was steady but uncertain. While Heckle lived to stir up mischief, Jeckle was a quiet soul. His favorite moment came when I'd set out a bowl of water. He would leap into it immediately, splattering, flapping, soaking himself with unfiltered delight. It was the one time he seemed as wild as his brother.

And then came the night I let them stay out. They'd grown restless. The call of the wild was stronger than the comfort of the porch. I left the cage open and let them decide.In the morning, Jeckle was gone. No feathers, no signs of struggle, just gone. I never saw him again. But the owls in that part of the jungle are big, fast, and silent. I don't think he stood a chance. It hurt, he wasn't just a bird, I had raised him, fed him, watched him bathe like a child playing in the tub. His absence was quiet, but sharp.

Heckle stayed for a while longer. But not alone. He joined up with a little gang of five young toucans, wild-born and wild-hearted. They traveled together like a squad of rowdy teens. They'd hang out in the canopy above my house, making a

racket, showing off, tossing fruit at each other. Heckle would still call to me now and then, from a branch just out of reach. But he no longer landed on my arm. He no longer needed to, and that to me was the goal. I didn't raise these birds to keep them, I raised them to return them.And though I lost Jeckle, I like to think he had at least one night of freedom under the stars. As for Heckle? He's probably still out there flying with his gang, slapping some poor monkey in the back of the head, laughing in that echoing toucan voice only the jungle understands.

Author's Note

Not every rescue ends the way you hope. I did everything I could for both of those birds, but sometimes nature has the final word. Jeckle was a sweet little soul, gentle, quiet, and easy to love. I wish he'd had more time. But part of living in the jungle is learning you don't get to control how long something lasts, only how well you care for it while it's in front of you. As for Heckle, he figured it out. He learned to fly, to join his own kind, to become exactly what he was meant to be. That's all I ever really want for any of them.
　—Mike

Chapter 5

Bubba

Bubba came into my life in the summer of 2003, delivered in a mayonnaise jar. I still remember it like it was yesterday. A friend of mine had found a tiny ball of fur along the side of the road. He was maybe six inches long, all legs and nose, barely alive. The friend handed me the jar and said, "I figured you'd know what to do."

The reason my friend brought the mayonnaise jar with Bubba inside to me was because I had rapidly been developing a reputation as the go to guy when wild animals with problems were found, and since I had had some experience volunteering in wildlife sanctuaries on the Prairie of Colorado, I knew the basics of wildlife rehabilitation on the Prairies of North America, but now I was in the jungles of Central America, hoping that the same techniques would apply.

Bubba was a Pizote, the local name for a Coatimundi. In English, people call them coatimundis or coatis, but down here in Costa Rica, they're known as Pizotes. They travel in troops, sniffing through the underbrush for fruit, insects, roots, anything they can scavenge or catch. They're curious, clever, and full of attitude. But Bubba was alone, which meant one thing, he'd been abandoned by his troop. Whether it was illness, weakness, or just bad luck, I don't know, but he wouldn't have lasted another day out there.

Luckily, I had goat's milk in the fridge. That stuff is liquid gold for young mammals cows' milk can kill small animals, but goat's milk is gentle, close to what many wild species can digest. I warmed it up, got Bubba hydrated, then fed him slowly, one tiny drop at a time. He took to it immediately. That was the start of it all.

He lived in a warm basket near my bed for the first few weeks. His fur was soft and wiry, his eyes too big for his face, and his nose twitchy with curiosity even before he could walk well. I knew early on he wasn't just going to survive, he was going to thrive.

And he did. What followed was years of companionship, mischief, and the kind of loyalty most people only expect from dogs. Bubba became more than a rescue, he became family.

Chapter 6

Bubba Meets Jerry and Tony

I lived on that mountain in Lagunas for eleven years, and during that time, I shared the hill with a revolving cast of creatures, rescued dogs, squirrels, possums, birds, and at one point, seven dogs all at once. But if you asked anyone who visited, there was always one name they remembered: Bubba.

About a year after Bubba came into my life, two of my closest friends Jerry and Tony came down to visit. They'd heard all the stories. They wanted to meet the wild thing in the flesh. I warned them, "He's not real big on strangers," I said. "And he's getting rowdier by the week." But they were curious, so we set up on the patio to make the introduction. It was a quiet, open space with a low coffee table in the middle, four chairs, and a hammock strung up between two posts. Along one side were big glass sliding doors that led into the house. The jungle pressed in beyond the patio like a green wall. Jerry and Tony sat down, grinning like this was going to be fun.

I went to get Bubba. Now, at that age, Bubba was still figuring out how strong he was. He wasn't aggressive with everyone, but he wasn't exactly tame, either. His favorite game was a chaotic one: climb the back of the chair closest to the hammock, launch into the hammock with a growl, roll around like he was in a bar fight, then drop to the floor, sprint back, and repeat.

When I brought him out, he spotted Jerry and Tony right away. He stared at them measuring, uncertain. But for the first few rounds, he just did his thing, leap, roll, growl, sprint, again and again. It almost looked like he was showing off. But then his growls got deeper. His play stopped looking like play. He sat in the hammock longer between each round, staring straight at Jerry and Tony—no longer bouncing, just growling, eyes locked. Jerry and Tony started to feel the energy began to change and were looking tentatively at each other, Bubbas growls became deeper.

That's when I said, "Okay. Time to go inside." They laughed—until they saw Bubba's face. Then they agreed. But it was too late. As Jerry and Tony stood up to make their exit, Bubba dropped from the hammock like a predator out of a tree. His prey had made the mistake of attempting to flee, and now it was on. He hit the ground and charged. I could tell instantly they weren't going to make it to the door in time. Then Jerry, cool under pressure, pulled a move I'll never forget. Straight out of a James Bond or Indiana Jones movie in one smooth motion he whipped off his hat and flung it to the ground in front of Bubba like a cowboy distracting a bull. It worked. Bubba pounced on the hat like it owed him money tearing it to shreds with those claws of his, growling and snorting like a tiny jungle demon.

Jerry and Tony made it to the glass doors but in their panic, they tried to go through at the same time and got stuck. Shoulders wedged, elbows flying, two full-grown men jammed in a doorway like a slapstick comedy sketch. I could barely stand. I was laughing so hard I couldn't breathe. Meanwhile, Bubba finished annihilating the hat. He looked up. His targets were stuck. He charged again. Claws hit the glass just as Jerry and Tony popped free, tumbled inside, and slid the patio door shut behind them.

They stood there panting, wild-eyed, sweating through their shirts. Bubba stood outside, eyes still blazing, nose against the glass like a creature in a horror movie, frustrated that the prey had escaped. Eventually, when I stopped laughing, I scooped him up and carried him back to his enclosure. He didn't resist, he'd won the game. And that hat? May it rest in pieces. But Jerry's move? That hat toss saved the

day. If he hadn't done it, they both would've left with a
souvenir carved into their shins.

Chapter 7

Bubba Meets Hollywood

By the time Bubba was three years old, he was no longer that fragile ball of fur in a jar—he was a full-grown adult male pizote. That means strong, territorial, and very opinionated. He still tolerated me, but anyone else? They were potential threats. Or targets.

So when my friend Quetzal, who was the developer of Costa Rica's biggest reptile emporium, called me up and said a host from Animal Planet was at his place, doing a segment for a TV show and wanted to meet Bubba, I had serious reservations. "He wants footage of something other than reptiles," Quetzal explained. "He heard about Bubba and thinks it could make a great segment." "Did you tell him Bubba's nickname is Freddy Krueger's cat" I asked. Quetzal laughed, "he's been warned." "Well, who is this guy?" I asked just out of curiosity and was informed that he was an animal planet show producer who was trying to make a pilot to sell to the animal planet network. "He's a pro," Quetzal said. "He can handle it." Famous last words.

The host, let's call him Hollywood, showed up with Quetzal and a full film crew of about five people. They had cameras, boom mics, backpacks, and bright smiles. Hollywood

21

himself was a brash loud South African, who didn't really want to hear anything about Bubba being dangerous. Bubba meanwhile was in the large enclosure I'd built for him in my backyard, about 40 feet long, 20 feet wide, and 10 feet tall, filled with logs to tear apart, a sheltered place to sleep, and everything he needed to stay wild but safe.

But Hollywood wasn't interested in filming Bubba through the fence. He wanted interaction. "I really wouldn't recommend that," I told him. "He's not a pet. He doesn't like strangers. Especially not ones holding strange looking electronic gear." Hollywood waved it off. "I'll be careful." I kept thinking to myself, 'This just keeps getting better and better. I shrugged, and told Hollywood, "Okay. But if something goes sideways, that's on you."

"This is when Jerry who is standing next to me on the patio, here on his yearly visit, heard me say I'm going to let Bubba out. He immediately headed for the stairs to the upstairs patio, slamming the door behind him safe from Bubba. I brought Bubba out to the front of the house. Hollywood and the crew waited at the bottom of the hill about an 80 yard stretch down a steep slope to a small grove where my machete guy had cleared the brush. Bubba was just grubbing in the dirt around my feet. so I yelled "make a little noise so he knows you're down there."

As soon as Bubba saw them, everything changed. His fur puffed out, and he froze stiff as a board at first, then he growled and launched. He tore down that hill in long low bounds, snarling like a beast twice his size. From the house, I heard the crew start panicking. "Oh my God, what the hell is that?! Is he coming at us?! He is, he's coming at us!"

Once the panicked film crew realized that fact they started looking for a place to hide problem was, there was no place to hide, and Bubba was closing fast. Hollywood on the other hand, stood his ground for about ten seconds. then his smile faded, and he turned to flee. But it was too late. Bubba was ten feet away and closing fast, then he leapt. He hit Hollywood square in the back like a clawing, biting backpack from hell, scratching, and snarling as the crew screamed and scattered. Cameras dropped, people ran, it was chaos. And through it all, came the roaring laughter of Jerry from the patio up at the house on the hill behind us.

I came charging down the hill, but Bubba spotted me before I got there. He dropped off Hollywood's back and disappeared down the hill and into the jungle. When I got to the crew, two were crying and the other two were peeling Hollywood's shirt off, bloody and torn. Amazingly, he wasn't seriously hurt. A lot of scratches, a few deep ones, but no real damage.

Then came the best part. "That was amazing!" Hollywood roared, grinning. "Please tell me you got that on film!" The allegedly experienced wildlife cameraman looked stricken. "No. i've never been attacked like that. We were running looking for a place to hide." Hollywood's face fell. Then he exploded. "That was the best footage we could've ever had, and you missed it?!" I tried not to laugh, but Jerry up on the hill wasn't making any attempt to hold it back, and he was literally roaring with laughter.

I started heading around the hill to intercept Bubba, knowing he always circled back through a trail down to the lower road. But before I made it a hundred feet, I heard someone shout, "O my God he's coming back!" I sprinted back to find Bubba charging out of the jungle and up the hill, this time, eyes wild, tail flared, and by the time I got there he had herded the entire crew into a loose circle and began circling them, low and slow, like a predator. The youngest member of the film crew was Literally crying. "Please! Help! Get him away from us," but Hollywood was trying to provoke another incident with Bubba, still upset that the film crew had missed the first attack.

I waded in, got close enough, grabbed his tail, and scooped him up like an angry toddler. He wriggled and grunted but didn't fight me. I carried him back to his enclosure and latched the gate. And in the distance at the bottom of the hill, I could hear Hollywood screaming at his film crew. Hollywood never came back. But the story? That one stayed with everybody.

Chapter 8

Jerry

Some people drift through your life like a breeze. Jerry came through like a freight train with bib overalls, a booming laugh, and the kind of presence you don't forget. We'd known each other since high school. Back then, Jerry had a reputation. They called him "Animal" because he had a habit of tearing through the middle of town on his old motorcycle, doing wheelies in full bib overalls, red-brown hair blowing in the wind, engine howling like a beast, no helmet, no hesitation, just Jerry.

Years later, when he found out I was living in Costa Rica, he didn't ask questions, he just showed up. That first visit was during my very first year in Lagunas. And then he came back every single year. Jerry wasn't tall, but he was big, about 300 pounds, and he carried it with confidence. His vivid reddish-brown hair and matching beard gave him a larger-than-life look, and his laugh could roll down a hill and shake the trees. He had a sharp, dry wit, and he never missed a chance to say something outrageous if it would make you spit out your drink.

He didn't come down to surf or go on jungle hikes, he came to hang his hammock near mine on the beach near the banana bread table, and chill in the sun. He became a presence on the mountain as well, more than once dressing up as Santa

Claus for the local kids, and he was perfect, the beard, the belly, the booming voice, they loved him, and so did the adults. He didn't just look the part, he played it with heart. When Jerry came to town, I knew life was about to get loud, ridiculous, and unforgettable.

There are a lot of Jerry stories, some wild, some hilarious, some that make you shake your head and grin. And every one of them deserves a place in this book..

Chapter 9

The Bridge at 1:00 AM

Every year, Jerry came to Costa Rica like a seasonal migration. And every year, something happened we'd never forget. This time, it was the bridge. He called to give me his arrival details, Juan Sanataria International Airport, 11:00 p.m. He asked if we were getting a hotel in San José or heading straight to Lagunas. We looked at each other, shrugged, grinned and chose the adventure.

It was rainy season, and the drive from the airport to my place was about four hours, part paved highway, part jungle road, and all of it soaked from days of storms. I picked him up in my small, single-cab Toyota truck, and off we went into the night. Around 1:00 a.m., we were deep in it. The highway had long since vanished behind us. We were crawling through muddy backroads, headlights bouncing off the rain-slick leaves. The jungle pressed close on our left side and the ocean was 200 meters to our right, and ahead of us was a suspension bridge over a wide rushing river.

Then we reached it. One of those old suspension bridges long, narrow, and barely held together with bolts and boards. It had no side rails, no lighting. Just a path of loose wooden planks stretched over a black pit of rushing water supported by old beams, salvaged from old buildings and crumbling concrete pillars. We eased onto it slowly. The bridge groaned under the weight of the truck.

Halfway across, everything went wrong. With a loud crack, the front wheels dropped straight through the bridge. The truck slammed down, its frame resting on the main beam of the bridge. Both front tires were now spinning helplessly in mid-air, ten feet above the rain swollen river, The rear tires still clung to the planks behind us. We were stuck. Suspended. And dead in the middle of a collapsing bridge. headlights pointing downward at about a 45° angle, illuminating the river of death just below us. Another vehicle had pulled up behind us—a few Ticos in a small car. They stopped short of going onto the bridge and got out, watching from a distance in the illumination of their headlights. Nobody was crossing until we figured this out.

I stepped out to look. It wasn't good. The truck was balanced like a teeter-totter, rocking slightly in the rain, front end down, wheels hanging. The only thing holding us out of the river was the frame resting on the beams. I crawled out to get as good as look as possible under the truck, But I didn't see any damage. Then I remembered that I had: four-wheel drive low. And what I also had: a 300-pound friend wearing camouflage bib overalls.

I lowered the tailgate and said, "Jerry, I need you to sit right here. Dead center. Your job is to hold the back end down while I back us out." He didn't ask questions. He climbed on and settled in like a boulder. I eased it into 4WD low, released the clutch slowly—and the truck backed out smooth as butter. The front tires slowly climbed back onto the planks like they were retracing their steps. Problem one: solved. Now came the next part, fixing the bridge.

I backed the truck up far enough to get clear of the break. Then, I stepped out into the rain, crouched low, and the pitch blackness only lit by my headlights,I straddled one of the main beams with a leg on either side. I slid forward slowly, inch by inch, until I reached the spot where the boards had shifted. Carefully, I repositioned the planks, locking them back into place. Then I crawled back to the truck, climbed in, and we tried again. This time, we made it.

As we rolled off the far side of the bridge, headlights lit us up like a stage, and the Ticos waiting there started cheering and clapping, calling out in Spanish, giving us thumbs up.

Jerry, still soaked from the tailgate, gave them a big wave. We continued the rest of the way home in the rain, mud-splattered, exhausted, and high on the thrill of having cheated disaster. And from that night forward, every single time Jerry came to visit, we told that story again. Word for word, board for board. Because you never forget the night the bridge tried to take you, and your big buddy in bib overalls saved the day.

Author's Note

That night could've gone a hundred different ways. But that's the thing about living in the jungle, you don't always get to plan how things unfold. You just respond, adapt, and lean on the people you trust. Jerry wasn't just comic relief. He was ballast, literally, that night and in life.

Chapter 10

D.A.W.G.

It didn't take long after I set up the banana bread table to notice something was wrong. Not with the bread. Not with the weather. With the dogs. There were a lot of them, beach dogs, mangy, sun-bleached, limping through the sand, sleeping in gutters, living off scraps from tourists and the kindhearted locals. Many had no owners, and some unfortunately had no future. They were constantly reproducing, sick, hungry, and covered in fleas and ticks. And while I was finding homes for puppies as fast as I could, I knew deep down it wasn't enough. This wasn't a rescue problem, it was a population problem. And because I knew I couldn't just sit there and watch it keep happening.

I decided to do something about it. I formed D.A.W.G., the Dominical Animal Welfare Group. My mission was simple: spay and neuter every beach dog I could catch and every dog a local would let me take. But there was a problem, the locals didn't see the point in paying to "fix" a dog. So I eliminated the problem. I went door to door, walking into shops, surf schools, restaurants, and anyone who knew me from the banana bread table, and I asked for help, donations, ten bucks, twenty, whatever they could give, and to my surprise, they came through, generously.

Next, I struck a deal with Fernando, the town vet, and a colleague of his from a neighboring pueblo. I told them I'd cover the costs if they'd drop their price. They agreed, and just like that, we had a spay-and-neuter operation. I started catching dogs one by one. Friendly ones, at first, then the tougher ones. I'd show up with a leash, a treat, a little sweet talk, and off we'd go to the clinic. But it wasn't enough. So we went bigger.

We began holding three day clinics, and pop-up veterinary setups in borrowed homes. I'd ask a friend or acquaintance to let us take over their house, clear out a living room, and set up operating tables. The first clinic did 60 dogs in 3 days, the next 85, and word spread. Locals started bringing their own dogs. Tourists started showing interest in adoptions. And I made it easy: I handled the bonding, while my vet friends handled the paperwork. We got the government permits, passports, and export approvals.

In all, I sent over 30 puppies to the U.S. with kind-hearted travelers. Many more were adopted locally, right here in Costa Rica. Within a couple of years, Dominical changed. There was a moment, brief but real, when you could walk the beach and not see a single stray dog. Except one, his name was Guapo.

In Costa Rican Spanish, guapo means "handsome." And this scrappy, snaggletoothed, barrel-chested mutt owned the name like royalty. I met him on my very first trip to Costa Rica before I ever moved there. I was sitting at a restaurant when he came right up to me and begged for a piece of my hamburger. He had this crooked little underbite, one cloudy eye, and a face full of character. He looked like he'd been in a hundred fights and won most of them. but the truth was

Guapo was all about peace and tranquility. Guapo was a legend.

By the time I launched the banana bread table, Guapo and I were already friends. But after that, we became something more. Every morning, he'd be waiting. I'd set up the table, and there he'd be, front paws stretched, back arched, tail swishing. His way of saying, "We working today, or what?" He'd stay by my side all day. And when I packed up and left, he'd wander off to the San Clemente bar and crash under a table. He lived exactly how he wanted to live. He was the last of the old guard. Eventually, I got help from a dedicated volunteer named Vicky who came on board along with a local Tica whose energy helped keep things rolling. But the real game changer was a woman named Shanell Parker.

Shanell showed up with fire in her eyes and a clipboard in her hand. She had organization, vision, and the will to build something bigger than I could ever manage alone. I was already neck deep in wildlife rescue, and it was clear if D.A.W.G. was going to survive and grow, it needed someone like her. So I passed her the torch. Shanell moved the group a few miles south to Uvita, changed the name to Domestic Animal Welfare Group (keeping the same acronym), and moved the whole operation into a building shared with the local vet. And she took it to the next level.

Under her care, D.A.W.G. became one of the largest spay-and-neuter and dog rescue operations in all of southern Costa Rica. it still exists today. And every time I think of it, I think of Guapo, the first to show up, and the last to leave.

Author's Note

There's a special kind of pride that comes from helping animals who can't speak for themselves. I didn't set out to become the guy rescuing dogs on the beach, I just saw something broken and decided to try and fix it. But what started as a few leashes and some donations turned into a mission that I never expected.

Guapo was the spirit of that beach. He didn't need rescuing, he was already free. But he reminded me every day why I was doing the work. He was a large part of the reason. Shanell Parker deserves all the credit in the world for what D.A.W.G. became. She took the seed I planted and grew a forest. If there's one thing I learned from that chapter of my life, it's this: you don't need a big plan to make a big difference. Sometimes all it takes is a table and a dog with an underbite — Mike

Chapter 11

A Golden Opportunity

As the days wore on at the banana bread table, each one seemed more perfect than the last. They blended together, sunrise to sunset, week to week, month to month, until the years slipped past in a golden haze of morning routines, afternoon baking, and an overwhelming sense that life was exactly as it should be.

Around the seven year mark, I introduced something new to the table: beef jerky. At first people gave it a funny look. Nobody in that part of Costa Rica had really seen jerky Colorado style But I handed out free samples anyway and as soon as they tasted it, everything changed. They couldn't get enough. My tiny single-tray dehydrator couldn't keep up with demand. So, I had someone bring me two larger dehydrators, and a vacuum sealer, and I set up a whole system. before a month had passed, I had it in three supermarkets up and down the coast and was selling it faster than I could make it.

Then came the phone call. It was from a friend of mine, a man named Arno, who spent part of the year in New York but owned a large jungle property in Costa Rica called Finca Florida. He had heard me talk about my time gold panning in Colorado and wanted to hire me to do a gold survey on his land. At this point, I should say that my gold panning experience was simply in the form of a weekend Hobby, find a little color type experience, but I did understand a little bit about prospecting and how to find places where gold might be.

His property was nestled deep in the jungle on the Osa Peninsula, one of the most wild areas of Costa Rica and famous for having gold in every river, Finca Florida was located about 25 miles downriver from the town of Sierpe, the trip would take us along the Rio Sierpe. Until it connected with the Rio Terrialba which eventually flowed into Drakes Bay. Finca Florida was located on the south side of the river about a half a mile before the river emptied into Drakes Bay. Adventure? Jungle? Gold? You'll never need to ask me twice for something like that. It meant time away from the banana bread table, but it was just too good to pass up.

I brought along my friend Sasha, a local legend in Dominical—bouncer, artist, party guy—and fluent in Spanish, which helped us strike a good deal with a riverboat captain. We loaded our gear and set off down the Rio Sierpe, winding through a jungle river that felt straight out of the Amazon. The water teemed with caimans, the trees pulsed with life, and birds of every color filled the sky. When we arrived at Finca Florida, I was blown away.

There was a magnificent lodge built from tropical hardwoods, tree trunks and limbs forming organic shapes, all wrapped in elegant architecture. Four cabanas lined the hillside, each with flower-lined steps. The landscaping was pristine, groomed by a single elderly man named Juan, probably in his nineties, who maintained the entire property by himself. It was surrounded on all sides by Corcovado National Forest, no roads, no electricity lines, no neighbors.

Just pure untouched jungle. We settled into our cabanas that afternoon, ready to begin our search for gold.

The next morning, we had jerky and granola for breakfast and set off with our map, heading to the streams that cut across Arno's property. Along the way, we passed a group of scattered homes, not a village exactly, but families living deep in the jungle with modest houses and trimmed lawns, supported by the bounty of the river.

That day, we didn't find much but we saw a few big snakes and a sounder of wild pigs (thankfully uninterested in us). I tried a few pans with my gold pans bought from a gringo moving out of Costa Rica, and turned up nothing.

That night, as we sat on the porch sipping local liquor, we gazed across the river at Violin Island. It wasn't really an island by typical standards as it was surrounded by miles of mangrove swamp, making it inaccessible by land and mysterious in every sense of the word. Soon we heard, "¡Oye! ¡Oye!" echoing from the jungle behind us. A local man appeared, lugging a burlap sack full of massive, fist-sized clams. He had come to sell them and probably to see who the two strangers were. We bought the whole sack and chatted with him for a long while.

He told us stories of Violin Island, how locals refused to go there because of its dense snake population, some said it had more snakes than any other place in Costa Rica. He spoke of ghosts guarding the rumored treasure of Sir Francis Drake, hidden deep in a cave on the island's rocky edge. He told us of a sorcerer named José who lived alone on the island and was feared by everyone. And he told us about the gold.

Violin Island, he claimed, held one of the richest untapped gold deposits in Costa Rica. The biggest gold nugget ever found in the country, 19 kilos, was discovered there and now sits in the national museum in San José. But mining was limited to hand tools only by law. No machinery, no roads, and no place for the faint of heart.

The next day, Sasha and I headed out in a new direction, deeper into the forest. Within minutes we came across a 6-foot terciopelo (Fer-de-lance) the biggest I'd ever seen. That's when you realize this isn't just an adventure, it's survival.

I found a bend in a creek and tried a few pans. A flash of gold glinted in the pan, just a trace, but enough to get excited. We mapped the spot, kept going, and eventually found another small inlet with even more color. It wasn't enough to make us rich, but it was enough to say there was gold here. We logged it for Arno, packed up, and spent our final evening marveling at the jungle sky.

The next morning we radioed Sierpe for a water taxi and rode back up the river past the mangroves, past the caimans, until we reached my truck.

Because after all that, I still had jerky to deliver.

Chapter 12

The Sorcerer of Violin Island

After our trip to Finca Florida, we rolled back into Dominical
and as I expected, every one of my jerky customers was
completely sold out, so I got back to work. I spent the next two
days making a fresh batch, bagging it all up, and then driving
around to restock the stores. Once the last delivery was made,
I figured it was time to call Arno and give him a full report.
He'd given me a map of Finca Florida before the trip, so I
wanted to show him exactly where we'd found traces of gold.
Then I could go back to my relaxed life of selling jerky,
enjoying the beach, and maybe knocking back a few beers
occasionally.

That evening around six, I pulled up to Arno's place with
the map in hand. He was happy to see me and even more
interested in what I had to show him. But I could tell there was
something else on his mind. That look in his eye told me this
visit wasn't just about gold. When Arno was cooking up
something, it usually meant another wild idea and that always
meant another adventure. He thanked me for the information
and swore me to secrecy about the gold. Then he said he'd be
in touch. Sure enough, about ten days later, my phone rang.
Arno had a whole new plan and this one was a beauty.

He wanted me to head back to Finca Florida, but this time, I was to cross the river the next morning and visit Violin Island. The mission was find the man named José, known locally as "the sorcerer" and try to strike a deal with him to set up a small scale, tourist-friendly gold panning operation on Violin Island. Arno had the idea that eco-tourists staying at his lodge would love taking a boat across the river, meeting a local character, and trying their hand at finding gold. It sounded crazy and exciting. Best of all, he was providing the boat this time, so I wouldn't have to charter one.

I'd drive to Sierpe, and the boat would be waiting. I'd take it downriver, cross over to Violin Island, meet José, and if all went well cut a deal. And Arno was even going to pay me. Sounds like a piece of cake... once again famous last words. But that was an offer I couldn't refuse.

I had about a week to prepare, so I used the time to do a little research on Violin Island and recruit someone to come with me. My first choice was my friend Quetzal. Quetzal was an American who'd been living in Costa Rica longer than I had. A self-taught herpetologist, he ran Reptilandia, a reptile park near Dominical that was probably the most impressive collection in southern Costa Rica. He spoke perfect Spanish, had a fearless attitude toward snakes, and an uncanny ability to spot them where no one else could. We'd done a couple of reptile collecting trips together before, and I trusted him completely. I figured he'd jump at the chance to explore an island rumored to be crawling with snakes and I was right.

The next morning, we met at my place, piled into my truck, and headed for Sierpe. We arrived early, so we grabbed breakfast at the Sierpe Café, Gallo Pinto, fried eggs, sausage, tortillas, and carne en salsa. While we finished our second coffee, Arno pulled up. Right behind him came Walter, the boat's owner, towing a 16-foot skiff with a 25-horsepower Evinrude. We launched the boat using the excuse for a ramp they had there, got some quick instructions from Walter, and waved goodbye to Arno. It was a pristine morning blue skies, calm water, no wind. We glided down the tributary into the main river, the jungle rising up on both sides, thick and green.

Birds of every shape and sound called from the trees. We passed the occasional wooden pier and modest huts where families had carved out a life from the jungle. Caymans sunned themselves on narrow beaches where the banks allowed it.

The trip downriver took about two hours, but it felt like a dream. By the time we reached Finca Florida, the sun was high, and the place was as beautifully maintained as ever. The old caretaker had kept every path trimmed, every corner swept. We settled in for the evening, relaxed in the cabinas, and readied ourselves for the morning's mission.

Arno had arranged for a local guide to meet us across the river at 9:00 a.m. The plan was simple: cross over to Violin Island, find José's camp, and make our pitch. The morning started smooth until we got to the meeting spot and found it completely empty. We waited an hour. No one came.

It was disappointing and a bit frustrating. But we weren't ready to give up. We began exploring the mangrove channels, hoping to find another way onto the island. Eventually, we stumbled upon a small fishing family living on a rise of land in the middle of the mangroves. One of the boys, around sixteen, said he knew where José was. We paid him a couple thousand colones and hired him as our guide.

After zigzagging through the mangrove waterways, we reached a muddy bank with a faint trail leading inland. We pulled the boat ashore and followed the path.

From the moment we set foot on Violin Island, Quetzal started spotting snakes. "There's one... and another... and one in the tree." I'd look and eventually see them—always after he pointed them out.

The place was alive with reptiles. But Quetzal wasn't fazed in the least. He was in his element. As we hiked further, the jungle began to change. The usual palms and ferns gave way to odd, unfamiliar plants—barrel-shaped stems, alien-looking blossoms. Our young guide explained that these were 'special plants' cultivated by José for his... 'purposes'. Eventually, the boy stopped and told us we'd have to wait. He went ahead to warn Jose, not to be startled. Apparently, he didn't appreciate unexpected guests.

We waited about 45 minutes before the boy returned, looking sheepish. He said Don Jose wasn't thrilled that we'd come, but had granted permission to enter his camp.

The place was unlike anything I'd ever seen. The camp sat at the base of a vertical rock wall. From that wall, a pipe jutted out, feeding clean water into a 50-gallon drum. A black plastic tarp covered a small shelter with an elevated bed. Scattered barrels held bananas, mangoes, and strange fruits I couldn't identify.

There was a makeshift breakfast bar with a few chairs. Don Juan welcomed us with a smile and motioned for us to sit. He was barefoot, wearing only shorts, and had the look of a man born from the jungle. His eyes were sharp, intense, but not unkind. The energy of the camp was... different, quiet heavy. Quetzal did most of the talking. His Spanish was far better than mine. We explained our proposal. Don` listened carefully. And when we were finished, he gave a small nod and politely said, "No."

He didn't want tourists all over his island. More importantly, he said the spirits that lived there wouldn't allow it. Still, he graciously accepted the bottle of honey we'd brought as a gift and sent us on our way. As we hiked back to the boat, our young guide said we were the first outsiders Don Jose had spoken to in a long time. Most people in the area were terrified of him. But he was also rumored to have performed some powerful healings.

It was still early, so Quetzal and I decided to take the boat closer to the ocean, land near the point, and do a little exploring. We walked out onto a wide shelf of rocks exposed by the tide. Every pool between the rocks was filled with fish, brilliant colors darting through the water. Deep red, bright yellow, electric blue. Some were large, some tiny, all perfectly adapted to their little pockets of seawater. It reminded me of the Shedd Aquarium in Chicago.

Eventually, we returned to the lodge, ate dinner, and rested up. The next morning, we cruised back upriver to meet Arno and Walter. They were waiting, boat trailer ready. We loaded the skiff, packed up, and once again pointed the truck toward Dominical. Those two days searching for a sorcerer, navigating jungle rivers, and wandering snake-covered trails stand out as some of the most unforgettable and best of my life. And somewhere on that strange little island, Don Juan still walks among the plants, the snakes, and the spirits.

Chapter 13

The Call That Changed Everything

When I got back to Dominical after the Violin Island trip, the jerky situation was exactly what I expected sold out everywhere. I hit the road the next day, loading up deliveries, restocking the stores, and getting the business humming again. I was spending less time at the banana bread table and more time producing and distributing jerky .That jerky had become my bread and butter, and the locals and the tourists we're buying it about as fast as I could produce it.

Once that was handled, I met up with Arno to give him a full report on our meeting with Don Juan. He was disappointed, sure but Arno was never the type to sit still in defeat. Without missing a beat, he pivoted to Plan B: a tourist gold recovery experience on his property at Finca Florida. "We'll set it up like a jungle adventure," he said. "People get to pan for gold and feel like treasure hunters." I told him I was in. He said he'd handle the permits and logistics and get back to me. But when the call came a few days later, it wasn't the update I expected.

"Mike," Arno said, "we're on hold. There's a shootout going on down near the property. Squatters versus police." I blinked. "Did you just say... a shootout?" Yep. A literal gunfight in the jungle. Over land. Over gold. Over who-knows-what. That put things in perspective real fast. The idea of leading tourists into the heart of that chaos with pockets full of gold flakes in a place where everybody from miles around knows what you're doing, and not a cop in sight suddenly didn't seem so charming. I let the dream go. The jungle had spoken. So I went back to jerky. Safe, delicious, profitable jerky.

I was sitting with my friends Steve and Dannia, just another mellow day, at first, then the phone rang, probably just another contact from the old banana bread table days. But this call would change everything, The man on the other end owned a development about 20 miles south of me, tucked up in the hills. We'd talked in passing a few times over the years about his idea to start a wildlife sanctuary. Now, he wasn't just talking, he wanted to move on it. He had investors. He had a vision. And he wanted me to design it, build it, and be the director.

Just like that, my whole world shifted. The universe was assigning me a new mission, it would be amazing and it would be difficult, and it immediately occurred to me that just like every other project I had undertaken in Costa Rica. I was gonna need a right hand native Costa Rican to help me navigate through the bureaucracy and permits that would surely be necessary with a project like this And wouldn't you know it—sitting right across from me was the best possible partner I could've hoped for: Dannia. She was sharp, bilingual, and studying to become a lawyer. She had charm, local connections, and a calm-but-commanding way of navigating bureaucracy. I looked at her made my pitch, and said, "You in?" She smiled. "Let's do it." The next morning, we fired up my old Toyota truck and headed to Ciudad Cortés to meet with

MINAE, the government agency that oversees animals, conservation, and environmental protection. These were the people who would either green-light the sanctuary… or bury it in red tape. Without these people on our side, the project was dead in the water, With them on our side. The project was protected.

I had no idea what to expect. When we walked into that office, we were greeted by a towering man in a government uniform who looked like he could've been an army colonel. He shook my hand, motioned us to sit, and after hearing our plan he looked us right in the eye, and said, "Where have you been? We've been waiting someone to open a sanctuary in Southern Costa Rica. Our need is desperate. A secretary came in and immediately started filling out paperwork and applications, and just like that the wheels were turning. Osa Santuario de Animales was born.

Then came the first test: the land itself. The sanctuary would be built on a remote mountaintop a solid 2 miles up a steep, gravel road that was more like a hiking trail than a driveway. At the top, a small spur led to a rounded hilltop with panoramic views of the ocean. That was the spot. Osa Santuario de Animales. The future home for rescues, releases, and redemption.

But first, we had to clear the site just a few trees and some brush but nothing could be touched without inspections. This was Costa Rica, after all. A land of natural beauty and paperwork.Tree permits. Soil impact reports. Flora studies. Fauna studies. Environmental impact evaluations. Building plan approvals. Meetings. More inspections. Signatures. Stamps. It took months. I spent more time in my truck than in my bed as we continued to jump through hoop after hoop, and at the same time, I had to keep my jerky customers stocked up but we kept pushing.

When we finally got permission to break ground, it felt like a miracle. And we didn't waste a second. I had designed the layout myself: A massive 80-foot by 40-foot cage, 20 feet high, split into two sections for large animals. Six smaller cages along the hill's edge, A dedicated enclosure for Bubba, of course, A central building with four covered cages beneath a roof perfect for the mid-sized rescues. A two-story main building, with a food prep kitchen and office below, and my living quarters upstairs, A converted shipping container, used for equipment storage, with a decked-out cabana built on top, complete with stairs and jungle views.

Between the buildings, we built a covered nursery area, lined with cages for the youngest and most fragile creatures. Wapping around the whole site, an 8-foot-high chain-link fence, topped with a solid wooden gate to keep everything, animal or human where it belonged.

Right as construction got underway, something big happened. I sold the house in Lagunas. After 11 years, it was time to let it go. I loved that place. I built a life there. But I knew in my bones this was the next step. When the main building was done, I packed up everything I owned, loaded Bubba into a crate, and made one final trip down that gravel road in lagunas. Osa Santuario de Animales had been born. And the real adventure... was just beginning.

Chapter 14

Osa Santuario de Animales

After months of grinding through the system—permits, inspections, hauling materials up a mountain, clearing jungle, wiring electricity, plumbing water, building cages, walls, roofs, and fences—it finally happened. Everything was done. Well... almost everything. We had one final inspection left. The big one. The visit from MINAE officials that would determine whether we could officially start accepting animals.

Dannia and I were both nervous. it all came down to this final inspection, either we had an animal sanctuary ready to function, or we had wasted a year of our lives.

We'd poured months of sweat and strategy into building this sanctuary. We knew the inspection would be thorough—MINAE doesn't mess around. They are the environmental and wildlife authority in Costa Rica, and if they weren't happy, it was back to waiting and paperwork. So when the two MINAE trucks pulled up that morning, my stomach was a little nauseous. But then I saw the back of the second truck, and everything changed.

Inside were a couple of crates. Animal crates. One held a parrot. Another, a small cage with something furry and twitchy. They didn't come just to inspect. They came to deliver. That's when it hit me: they already knew! They'd reviewed the reports, seen the photos, signed off on the blueprints—and they were bringing us our first official rescued creatures. We were in.

Here's how it works in Costa Rica: once MINAE delivers an animal to a sanctuary, the director—you're lookin at him—has to sign legal paperwork becoming the official custodian of that animal. Not a caretaker. Not a host. A full-blown, legally bound guardian. If that parrot bites a tourist or that monkey swings off into the town and bites the mayor's wife, guess who's on the hook? Each sanctuary is also assigned a government-accredited biologist. Ours was a guy named Franklin. He was a calm, capable man, he had a strong presence and a professional attitude, He'd visit from time to time to check on the animals and make sure the place was being run right. if he saw something that he thought wasn't correct needed to be fixed or had suggestions to make he did so, he was a valuable member of the team.

Now technically, it's illegal for anyone in Costa Rica to keep wild animals as pets. But "technically" is the key word. This is a country where parrots are in every tree, monkeys cross the road like squirrels, and people grow up surrounded by wildlife.

So what happens? They take in baby animals, parrots, monkeys, kinkajous, sloths, and raise them like pets. Sometimes it's because they found them abandoned. Sometimes they just want a jungle companion. But sooner or later, word gets out. Someone reports it. MINAE finds out. And then that animal is confiscated and if the stars align, delivered to a registered sanctuary like ours.

But here's the hard part: once a wild animal gets used to people, it loses its edge. If a monkey forgets to fear dogs, or a parrot sees humans as the only food source, that animal is unlikely to survive if released. It's heartbreaking, but it's the reality we dealt with. We worked mostly with parrots at Osa, especially the Amazon species. The one we saw most often was the red-lored Amazon, like Pete, our first parrot. We also received mealy Amazons, yellow-napes, the occasional macaw, and a steady flow of smaller parrots, parrotlets, and pericos.

Pericos, technically orange-chinned parakeets, were the most common. Tiny, bright green, sparrow-sized, and loud as hell. They were everywhere. People would cut down a tree and find a nest of bald, screeching chicks inside. Before long, someone would show up at our door with a cardboard box full of them. We raised them by hand. Fed them until they could eat on their own, preened their feathers, and when they were ready we released them. But they didn't always leave.

Every morning, I'd walk out of the house and get dive-bombed by a small cloud of green. A dozen pericos would land on my shoulders and head, shrieking for breakfast like they'd never eaten in their lives. That became the routine. Now, most of the pericos were released directly into the wild once they were strong enough to fly. But some weren't so lucky. We often received injured or crippled pericos, birds that couldn't fly, sometimes from birth, sometimes from bad handling or falls. For those, we built a separate cage just for them. A safe space, protected from predators, where they could still live in a small flock and feel part of something. The sanctuary was built with all of this in mind.

Our biggest cage. 80 feet long, 40 feet wide, 20 feet tall was split in half. One side housed the large adult parrots. The other side? That was for monkeys. It was critical to give them both space and security, while also keeping species separate when needed.

Smaller cages lined one side of the property. We had a nursery area for the babies, a row of enclosures for individual cases, a storage container for supplies, a food prep area, and my own modest quarters built above the office and kitchen. Everything was ready.

The MINAE team did their walkthrough. They checked the fences, the enclosures, the food prep stations. They asked a few questions, made a couple notes, and finally, nodded. We were approved. And just like that, they handed over our first official residents: Pete the Parrot, a red-lored Amazon with a big beak and a bigger attitude, Bobber, a little perico with a permanent head tilt and way too much confidence, and Felipe, a baby squirrel monkey, what the locals call a titi.

As I was settling the birds into their new homes, Dannia walked over to Felipe's crate.That was it. Her eyes softened. Her arms reached out. She scooped him up gently and started cooing in Spanish and English like a brand-new mom.

"Ohhhh, look at your tiny little hands...you are so precious, yes you are..."

She was gone. The maternal switch had flipped. And Felipe, being no fool, curled into her arms and soaked up every second of it. The sanctuary was officially alive. And it was only just beginning.

Chapter 15

The First Arrivals

Once the sanctuary officially opened, things went from quiet to chaotic in about three days. The word was out. MINAE had our paperwork. The cages were ready. And suddenly, it was like someone flipped a switch, animals started showing up fast. By the end of the first week, we already had a full cast of new residents: Coco, a white-faced monkey who immediately began trying to steal anything shiny; Harpo, a crested guan chick with big feet, pinfeathers, and nonstop squawking; and Whitey and Twitch, two baby Costa Rican squirrels with beautiful colors and big appetites.

We also had a couple more Amazon parrots with lungs like airhorns, and a brand-new clutch of nine baby pericos, still bald and squealing, delivered in a cardboard box that smelled like fear and fruit. It was already starting to feel like a real sanctuary. And then... Blossom arrived.

It was one of those perfect Costa Rican mornings, blue skies, birds chirping, warm breeze blowing through the palms, when I heard the familiar crunch of tires on gravel. The MINAE truck rolled up to the gate. Driving it was Danny, one of my favorite officers. A big, round, good-natured guy who always wore a smile and somehow made bureaucracy feel human. As he got out of the truck, I noticed his hands were cupped together gently, like he was holding something fragile. "Got a special one for you," he said, walking over. I leaned in. At first, I couldn't even tell what I was looking at. It was a small gray ball, barely breathing, curled up in his palms like a fallen pinecone. Then he placed it in my hands and I felt it move. Soft. Warm. Spiky. A baby porcupine. I blinked. "You've gotta be kidding." He grinned. "Less than a week old."

She was tiny. Her eyes were still closed. Her little belly was sunken in. She was cold, quiet, and way too still. I knew exactly what that meant, she'd been separated from her mother for too long. Dehydrated. Fading fast. I signed the intake papers, thanked Danny, and carried her inside like she was made of glass. She was a Mexican hairy dwarf porcupine, a tree-dwelling species with a prehensile tail and a body built for the canopy. Fully grown, they're maybe 12 to 14 inches long. But this one? She fit in the palm of my hand. I looked down at her and didn't even have to think about it. Her name was Blossom. And she couldn't be more than a few days old.

Now with newborns like this, time is everything. First step: rehydrate. With older animals, I could sometimes get away with baby electrolyte formulas or, in a pinch, even Gatorade. But baby mammals? They need water first, then goat's milk, period. Cow's milk will kill them. Goat's milk is the only safe option, easy to digest and gentle enough for all kinds of wild stomachs. I warmed up a bottle and gently touched it to her lips. She latched instantly. Started sucking hard. Made this low, satisfied grunting sound that gave me hope. She was maybe going to make it. But we weren't out of the woods yet.

With small mammals, you have to weigh them constantly twice a day, minimum. That's the only real way to know if they're improving. For the first three days, Blossom drank well, but her weight didn't change. That was bad. If a baby's not gaining, Something wasn't working.

I made a call to a friend at the Miami Zoo, a person I had met during my days at the banana bread table, someone I trusted. Told him what was going on. "Try blending a little banana into her milk," he said. "Boost her calories. Get her gut moving." So I did. Banana and warm goat's milk. A weird mix, but she loved it. And it worked. By day four, she was gaining weight. By day six, she had filled out. Her fur fluffed up. Her energy came back. She started climbing. Nosing around. Watching me. She was on her way.

Because Blossom had to be hand-raised from such a young age, her chances of being released into the wild were almost zero, she was too bonded, too humanized. But she didn't seem to mind. In fact, she acted like I was hers. She followed me wherever she could. If I stepped out of sight, she'd start calling for me, soft little cries that sounded almost like a cat. And when I picked her up? She'd flatten her quills. It was the most remarkable thing. All those barbed spines would go smooth, like a plastic shell, just so she wouldn't poke me. She knew. She was careful. Sure, every now and then I'd get a quill in the arm, but it was never on purpose. She never flared. Never bristled. She just wanted to be close. What Blossom loved most was to crawl into my lap, curl up like a dog, and be petted. For her, that was home.

I've worked with a lot of animals in Costa Rica. Some wild, some dangerous, some hilarious, some heartbreaking. But Blossom? She was something else. She was gentle, devoted, and smarter than most people would ever believe a porcupine could be. And from the moment she took that first drink of warm goat's milk she was in a safe place, but she would also never know freedom.

Chapter 16

Tubby the Tipisquenti

Not every animal came through MINAE, mostly they did. That was the standard process, the government delivers a confiscated animal, I sign the paperwork, and boom, we're officially in business. But other times? The jungle sent them a different way. Sometimes I'd get a phone call. Sometimes locals would just show up at the gate with a cardboard box or a

dog crate and a story that didn't quite add up. And sometimes, things I never saw coming. This was one of those times.

It started on a normal morning. I was inside the big parrot cage, doing the usual cleaning. Dannia was prepping food for the day's feedings when her phone rang. She picked up, listened for a moment, then looked over at me with an expression somewhere between confusion and disbelief. "It's the hardware store in Uvita," she said. "There's a Tipisquenti running loose in the aisles. A what? In English, it's called a paca—a jungle rodent the size of a small dog. Nocturnal. Vegetarian. Shy. Lives deep in the forest. also reputed to be the best meat in the world and completely protected by the government. Not exactly your average hardware store shopper. I grabbed my keys and hit the road.

The moment I pulled up to the store, something felt off. Pacas don't just show up in towns. They're animals of the deep jungle, quiet, elusive, rarely seen. So why was one pacing between paint cans and plumbing supplies in the middle of downtown Uvita? Then I saw him. The second I laid eyes on that animal, the whole story clicked into place. He wasn't wild. He was fat.

This was no jungle-dwelling animal. This was a domesticated paca who'd broken out of some backyard pen. He was well-fed, glossy, and slow. Real slow. A good 40 pounds—waddling up and down the tile aisles like a runaway Thanksgiving turkey. And the way he slid on the tile? I almost felt bad for him. He had no traction, no plan, no idea how to escape this shiny-floored nightmare. That's when it hit me, Tubby, and it stuck.

I chased him around for a few minutes, doing a awkward dance between lawn tools and bags of cement. Eventually got a net over him, wrestled him into a dog crate, and secured him in the back of my truck. Tubby was coming home. Now came the next question, where to put him?

During construction I had installed a big shipping container on the property as our central supply zone; tools, fencing, food bins, you name it. On top of that container, I'd built a cabina for Dannia, complete with a wide wooden deck that overlooked the jungle. Underneath that deck was a shaded area about 150 square feet. I had fenced it off with 4-foot chain link and lined the ground with big, round river rocks to discourage digging. It wasn't meant to be a permanent animal enclosure. But it was perfect for a big, burrowing, slow-moving rodent who needed space and safety. So I brought Tubby home, opened the crate, and let him walk out. Within minutes, he found a spot under the shipping container, started excavating like it was his full-time job. I tossed him a half bale of hay, and mouthful by mouthful, he pulled it all underground into his new den.

Tubby was home. He was happy. He was free. Everything was perfect. For about fifteen minutes. I had barely gotten him settled when I heard the rumble of a truck on the gravel drive and then, BANG BANG BANG on the front gate. I didn't need a crystal ball to know what was coming. I walked over, opened the gate, and there they were: two Ticos in farm clothes. Rough hands, rubber boots, the whole look. But they weren't ready for me. When they saw me gringo sanctuary owner, arms crossed, not smiling their whole tone changed. Gone was the aggressive pounding and shouting. Now it was, "Um... can we please have our Tipisquenti back?" I almost laughed.

Tubby had been theirs. No doubt. They'd captured him, fattened him up, and were counting the days until he hit the dinner table. But Tubby had other plans and somehow, fate (and a hardware store) brought him to me instead. I let them know the bad news. "Tubby's not going anywhere," I said. "I've already notified MINAE. He's now the legal property of the Costa Rican government. And just so you know, I've got your license plate." They didn't like that. They cussed me out, turned around, and drove off. But they didn't get their dinner back. Tubby the Tipisquenti stayed exactly where he was safe, full, and free to live out his life waddling under a deck in peace, right where he belonged.

Chapter 17

Population Explosion

When the doors of Osa Santuario de Animales finally opened, it didn't take long to realize what that MINAE official meant when he first looked at me and said: "Where have you been? We've been waiting for you." At the time, I thought he was just being nice but he wasn't, he was being literal, because the second we opened, the deliveries started fast and furious. Three, sometimes four times a week, MINAE trucks would roll in, tailgates full, cages rattling, animals wide-eyed. Turns out, they had a long list of confiscated animals they couldn't remove from illegal homes because they had nowhere to take them until we came along. And once we were open, all bets were off.

By the end of the third month, the place was buzzing. We had: over 20 Amazon parrots red-lored, mealy, yellow-naped, you name it. There was a revolving door of perico chicks, squealing and featherless, and nearly every cage filled with mammals ranging from bottle-fed babies to fully domesticated adults that would walk right up to you and ask for food. We had three of the four monkey species native to Costa Rica. White-faced capuchins? We had two: Coco, our queen of mischief and Pablo, a young male confiscated from drug smugglers so of course, that's what we named him these two white face monkeys were Dannia's personal babies. Squirrel monkeys? We had three: Felipe, who followed me from Lagunas, and Pepe rescued from a rusted backyard cage in Palmar Norte. They weren't going anywhere. Raised by humans, they had no jungle future. But here, they were safe.

Then there was Lulu. A baby howler monkey, beautiful and clingy as all get-out. Every day, she'd attach herself to the back of my neck like a furry little backpack. And if I tried to put her down? She'd scream like a fire alarm. She made hammering nails and cleaning cages a bit more complicated.

There was Gomer, the tamandua an arboreal anteater the size of a small dog, with a long nose, slow movements, and zero interest in hurrying. One of my all-time favorites. There was Sweetie, a soft, golden-eyed kinkajou who'd barely survived a dog attack. We cleaned her wounds, bottle-fed her goat milk, and brought her back to health. Sweetie was gentle and loved to cuddle but she was nocturnal, which meant bedtime for us was party time for her.

We had squirrels, not your backyard squirrels from the States. These had five colors: white, yellow, brown, beige, and black. Absolutely stunning. There were raccoons, surprisingly common, and plenty of babies raised by hand. There were possums, including: the fast, delicate four-eyed possums, the slow, fuzzy woolly possums, and the meat-eating, fast-as-hell zorros, Costa Rica's version of a predator possum.

Then there were the birds. The big flight cage held: Red-lored, mealy, and yellow-naped Amazons, two scarlet macaws one missing an eye from a BB gun, the other with all his tail feathers ripped out by his former owner (they don't grow back, so he'd never fly again). There was also white-capped pionus

and blue-headed pionus, called chucuyos by locals, several
red-fronted long-tailed parakeets, and a sky full of pericos,
many of which we'd raised and released and who never really
left. The place was alive. The sanctuary had taken on a rhythm,

a heartbeat.

Every day, Dannia and I woke up and dove into the routine. Food prep started early and again in the afternoon. Every animal had a different diet. Some needed fruit sliced a certain way. Others needed soaked kibble, blended veggies, or hand-fed formula. Dannia had it all memorized. She ran that kitchen like a drill sergeant, firm, precise, and unshakable. If volunteers were helping, she trained them. If not, she did it herself. She was a force of nature.

Meanwhile, I was everywhere; cleaning cages, prepping bottles, taking supply runs, logging animal intakes, feeding the babies (especially the ones that needed 3–5 feedings a day, including at 2 a.m.) I was also giving tours, and fixing every little thing that broke, which, in a jungle sanctuary, was a lot. We also had a vet from Palmar Norte who came once a week, or whenever we had an emergency. She was kind, sharp, and incredibly valuable. We leaned on her often.

And then there were the volunteers, especially the local women from the mountain community. Once trained, they became baby feeders, cage scrubbers, and sometimes, full-on animal moms. I handpicked three of them and taught them everything they needed to know to safely feed delicate babies. Their maternal instincts kicked in like clockwork. They never missed a feeding. Two of them even canceled their flights back to the States just to keep caring for the animals they had bonded with. Perfect.

Of course, most animals came to us already too domesticated to ever be released. Once a monkey or a parrot learns to rely on humans, forgets to fear dogs, or loses its natural instincts it's done. That's the reality. But once in a while... we got a shot. An animal would come in from the wild with a broken wing, a busted leg, or a concussion from a car hit or power line. If we could fix it, we would, and if they healed up and passed all the signs, we'd take them back to the exact spot they were found so they could find the food, the water, the place in the ecosystem they'd left behind. That was the best part of the job. But it was rare. Mostly, our job was permanent care. The animals kept coming, and we kept adjusting.

Then one afternoon, I was standing at the edge of the sanctuary, looking out at what Dannia and I had built. Listening to the birds, watching the monkeys, feeling that rare moment of satisfaction. And I heard it. The familiar sound of tires on gravel coming down the road.

Chapter 18

Chester and Festus

By now, the sanctuary had been operating for more than a year, and we'd built up a pretty wild little cast of characters. There was Sophia, the agouti what Costa Ricans call a guatusa. She looked like a guinea pig with stilts. Fast, alert, and totally at home digging tunnels under the sanctuary fence. She'd come to us half-grown and already domesticated, and we let her run loose inside the fence line. She claimed a corner of the property, dug herself a burrow, and kept mostly to herself like a tiny jungle landlord.

Then there was Buck, a whitetail deer fawn who arrived just a couple weeks old. We bottle-fed him until he grew into a confident, healthy young buck who roamed the sanctuary like he was the one in charge. We had Nigel the baby sloth, named after Animal Planet host Nigel Marven, who happened to visit one day and instantly fell in love with the little guy. And, of course, the usual crew: Bubba, Felipe, Tubby, and so many more that it would take a phone book to list them all.

The sanctuary was running like a well oiled machine. We were raising babies, doing releases, and giving a permanent home to the ones who couldn't go back. It was hard work, but it was working. Then came that familiar sound, MINAE rolling down the hill. And as always, I felt that mix of excitement and curiosity in my gut. What were they bringing this time? I didn't have to wait long.

As the truck pulled into the gate, I could see the officers already wearing that look, the one that says this is different. In the back of the truck were two enormous dog crates. And inside those crates? Two Geoffroy's spider monkeys. My jaw hit the floor. These were the big ones, long-limbed, agile, intelligent. The largest monkey species in Costa Rica. They can live over 30 years and stand nearly a meter tall.

The officers gave me the backstory. The two monkeys, both adults, had been kept near the Panamanian border for over 20 years, collared and tied to sticks in a yard. That was their life. No trees. No movement. Just a post, a collar, dirt floor, and whatever food was thrown their way. Now, suddenly, the only life they knew was about to change drastically.

One was 23 years old, the other one was 20. They were nervous, twitchy, unsure of the world, but they were here, and the moment I looked at them, the names came to me: Chester and Festus. If you grew up on Gunsmoke, you know exactly what that means. Chester and Festus were the quirky deputies. Always showing up at the wrong time. Loyal but a little unhinged. Perfect names I thought. MINAE explained: Chester had all his teeth and was pretty mellow. Festus had a reputation, agitated, unpredictable and someone had actually removed his teeth somewhere along the line. Brutal.

I brought them into the sanctuary and moved them straight into the big enclosure built just for cases like this. It had ropes, platforms, a high house, a natural water fountain, and plenty of room to swing, climb, and live. And that's when it started. They realized they were free. At first they hesitated, moved slowly, tentative, but then it hit them; they weren't on leashes, they weren't tied to a stick, they could move, and they did. They swung from rope to rope. Bounced off platforms. Climbed the walls. You could see it happen in real time twenty years of captivity melting off their bodies. That moment alone made the whole sanctuary worth it.

The next morning, I approached the cage to check on them while Dannia prepped food inside the kitchen. They came to the front of the enclosure calm, curious. I handed them raisins through the fence. No problem. They let me touch them. They touched me back. Everything seemed great. But I needed to know if I could safely enter the cage. It had to be cleaned daily. Food had to be delivered. I had to know: were they going to tolerate me inside? Or was this going to be a problem?

The enclosure was built with a double door system. I stepped into the entry chamber and closed the outer gate behind me. They didn't react. So I opened the inner gate and stepped inside. Chester and Festus approached, calm as ever. We interacted. I stayed alert. No issues. Very positive but enough for the first day.

As I backed into the entry chamber to leave, Festus followed me. That was an issue.I couldn't open the outer gate with him there, he'd escape. But he wouldn't go back into the main enclosure, either. He knew that door was his shot at freedom. So I reached out gently to nudge him back. That's when the whole situation went straight to hell. Festus screamed, and Chester came flying. He hit me like a fury. Bit me hard, once in the upper thigh, once in the forearm. He had teeth like a dog, big sharp canines. He tore into me before I could even react. I grabbed him by the upper arms, under his shoulders, and now we were locked together.

He had five points of contact: hands on my forearms, scratching me with long, dirty nails, his feet were wrapped around my waist, and his tail coiled tight around my torso. And me, I had two hands holding him back, barely. His face was inches from mine. His teeth were snapping. His eyes were wild. I couldn't get free. Couldn't throw him. Couldn't push him off. And I sure as hell couldn't run. Then I looked down. Blood soaked through my pants dinner-plate sized. My forearm was dripping, it was bad.

Dannia heard the noise and came out from the kitchen only to freeze in shock.She was panicked. Didn't know what to do. I knew I had to act fast. So I came up with a plan. The idea was to spin around, pick up momentum and fling Chester away from me. Even to me it didn't sound like much of a plan, but it was all I had so I tried it. To my surprise, he let go midair. He flew about ten feet, landed on all fours, and came right back. Teeth bared. Arms straight up.

I had no time to reach the gate. it was at this moment that I knew that I was in a serious situation. I didn't know how far this monkey was willing to take it, but I wasn't gonna make it easy for him. So I squared up. fully prepared to fight my way out of that cage if necessary. I looked him in the eyes. raised my fists and said out loud, " OK YOU MONKEY SON OF A B**** LET'S GO! And that's when everything changed.

He stopped. He looked into my face and saw something. He saw that I wasn't playing. I was scared—but I was serious. I was ready to fight my way out of that cage. And he backed down. He dropped his arms. And in that split second, I slipped out through the gate, slammed it shut, and locked it behind me. I walked into the vet room, soaked in blood. I bandaged myself up, stopped the bleeding, then I grabbed a beer.

It was a memorable day at Osa Santuario de Animales

73

Chapter 19

Gomer the Tamandua

The morning after the monkey attack, I woke up sore, bloodied, and stiff. I peeled back the bandages to inspect the damage, and yeah, no question about it, things were looking a little infected.

Now, a monkey bite isn't just any old scratch. Their mouths are loaded with bacteria. If you let one of those go, you're not dealing with a scar, you're dealing with sepsis, or worse.

I drove down the hill to the little clinic in Palmar Norte, where the local doctor gave me the once-over. My tetanus shot was still current, thank God, but he cleaned the wounds, gave me a grim look, and handed me a 10-day supply of antibiotics. No questions asked. He knew exactly what kind of wild stuff we dealt with up at the sanctuary.

With my arm wrapped, my thigh still pulsing, and a pack of meds in my pocket, I grabbed a bite and a few supplies before heading back up the hill.

As I turned the last corner up to the sanctuary, I saw the MINAE trucks waiting at the gate. Of course they were. This time they had something different, something special. In the back of the truck was a small wide eyed creature clinging to the corner of a kennel crate like it wasn't sure what planet it had landed on. I recognized it immediately; a Tamandua.

Now, a Tamandua isn't your average anteater. It's an arboreal species (lives the trees) and it looks like something between a sloth, a raccoon, and a prehistoric beast. About the size of a house cat, long claws, small snout, small teeth for grinding insects. This one was young—very young. Barely old enough to be weaned. They said it had been found sitting stunned in the middle of a road, no mother in sight. Someone scooped it up, passed it to MINAE, and now here he was, dropped at my feet like some ancient jungle puzzle I was supposed to solve. He needed a name, and the second I looked into those glassy black eyes it came to me: Gomer.

I scooped Gomer up and brought him into the kitchen. Dannia was already one step ahead of me. She had a warm bottle of goat milk ready to go. Now here's the thing: you can't just stick a regular bottle into the mouth of a Tamandua. Their mouths are tiny—narrower than a pencil. So we had to pull out one of our specialty bottles with a long, thin nipple built just for animals like this. I wasn't sure it would work.

But then Gomer surprised us. He latched on like a pro, sucking down the goat milk like it came straight from Mama Tamandua herself. It was a beautiful thing, that moment when you know he's going to make it. And I had no idea just how much I was going to fall for this little guy.

Goat milk got us through the critical window, but Gomer couldn't live on it forever. So I called in reinforcements, my contact at the Miami Zoo. They'd raised Tamanduas before. I needed the real deal.Here's what they gave me, the official Tamandua diet: 2 cups plain yogurt, ½ pound lean ground beef, 4 raw egg yolks, 1 cup of live jungle termites (easy—we had nests the size of pumpkins), ½ can of turkey-only cat food pâté (low fat only), 2 fresh sprigs of spinach, and the very important ingredient, 2 ounces of apple cider vinegar. Put the whole thing in the blender, cranked it on high, and let it liquify into what looked like something between a smoothie and a biology experiment.

It smelled… sharp. But Gomer loved it. More than that, he craved it. Especially the vinegar. I'd pour him a little dish of pure apple cider vinegar on the side, and he'd lap it up first, like it was dessert. Turns out, that's not just a preference, it's survival.

Tamanduas don't produce much stomach acid. In the wild, they get formic acid from the ants and termites they eat. In captivity, you've got to replace that missing acid, or they can't digest effectively without it, they can get bloated, sick, and possibly die.

That vinegar? It's not just helpful. It's vital. But that wasn't the only thing we had to watch. If a Tamandua gets something in its stomach it can't digest, it might try to vomit, and with a mouth that small it can't. They choke. They die. So their diet has to be perfec, no mistakes. And with Gomer, we were perfect. He grew stronger every day. More confident. More curious. And more bonded to me than I ever expected. He'd follow me around the sanctuary like a shadow. If I disappeared, he'd grunt and shuffle around until he found me again. And every time I saw him slurping down his vinegar cocktail, I was almost tempted to try it myself… but I never did.

Chapter 20

Trouble in Paradise

Running a wildlife sanctuary sounds like paradise, and in many ways, it was. But it was also expensive. Very expensive. When we first came to Osa Mountain, we had been assured of steady financial support through the other tourist ventures operating in the community, the water slide, the organic gardens, the mountain biking trails, an incredible butterfly garden, and most importantly, the zip-line. That zip-line wasn't just a thrill ride it was supposed to be our golden ticket. The sanctuary had been strategically placed at the end of the zip-line tour, just a hundred yards from where guests dismounted, and the plan, the promise, was that every guest would be offered the opportunity to walk directly into the sanctuary for a visit. But that's not what happened.

Instead, the zip-line operators actively discouraged their guests from coming through our gates. They told them falsely, that if they took a tour of the sanctuary, they'd forfeit their ride back down the mountain. Most guests didn't want to risk being stranded, so even as they stood at our gate, peering in with interest, some with their noses pressed against the chain link like kids at a zoo, they eventually turned away.

It was maddening. as well as suspicious. I had been promised foot traffic, ticket sales, and a partnership. What I got was isolation. I confronted the zip-line managers several times. Each time I was met with apologies, promises, and hollow reassurances that things would change. They didn't. Day after day, I watched potential visitors walk past our entrance, 5, 10, 20 at a time, and disappear down the mountain.

Now don't get me wrong, the sanctuary itself was thriving in spirit. Animals continued to arrive through MINAE, babies were raised, releases were made, and new cages were built. We were doing what we had set out to do. But the money wasn't coming in. I could see the numbers tightening. And tightening fast.

We tried everything: GoFundMe campaigns, school tours, flyers, social media, even a local radio spot. But the reality was setting in. Our location was just too remote. Too hard to access. And despite our efforts, the foot traffic just wasn't enough to sustain what we were doing.

Worse than that, far worse, was the knowledge that over 100 animals and birds, representing the wild heart of Costa Rica, were now depending on me. Every one of them had been rescued from trauma, abuse, abandonment, or confiscation. Without the sanctuary, these creatures wouldn't just be homeless, they'd be doomed. Many would be returned to the cruel conditions from which they came. Others wouldn't survive at all. The idea of the sanctuary going under wasn't just heartbreaking it was unthinkable. If these animals were going to have a chance, a real chance then the sanctuary had to move. It had to relocate to a place where people could get to it. Where tourism could support the mission.

It was time for Plan B.

Chapter 21

Plan B... Activated!

By the spring of 2014, the writing was on the wall. The sanctuary had been running for just over two years, and the financial walls were starting to close in. The startup money was gone. The occasional visitor was never enough to sustain the operation, especially when every trip up that brutal two km mountain road required four-wheel drive and a little faith.

For a long time, I had kept the sanctuary afloat using the profits from the sale of my house in Lagunas. But those funds were dropping fast. I could feel the slope under my feet getting slicker with every passing month. It was time to face the reality: we either found a new home, or the sanctuary, and the animals that had come to depend on it, would be in real trouble.

For the past two months, I had quietly been scouting for a new location. The list of requirements was long, but non-negotiable:

Enough land for proper enclosures

Far enough from the highway to keep things peaceful

Access to electricity and water

Easy enough for tourists to reach

And most importantly... I needed a sponsor. I had already burned through my resources building one sanctuary from the ground up. Doing it again was not going to be possible on my own dime. I started tapping into the network I had built over the years, from the banana bread table to my time in Dominical, and sure enough, offers began to appear. Unfortunately, so did red flags.

One offered location was barely more than a sloped hillside right on the highway, no privacy, no space. Dangerous for animals in the sanctuary. A total nonstarter. The other offer came from a man whose eyes lit up with dollar signs at the thought of hosting the sanctuary. To him, it was not a place for healing animals, it was a gold mine. That was a hard no. But the problem remained. The sanctuary had to move. Or it would not survive.

Then, one morning in early April, the universe cracked the door open. I was in the middle of admitting two more Red-Lored Amazon parrots and a pair of beautiful baby Costa Rican squirrels into the sanctuary. I signed the paperwork and named the squirrels Rocky and Nutcase, and two of our regular volunteers immediately scooped them up like they were newborns and rushed off to the nursery to give them their first taste of goat milk. Right then, there was a knock at the gate. When I opened it, two young women were standing there. I recognized them. They had passed by earlier with the zip-line tour. They told me they had refused the ride back down the mountain so they could stay and see the animal sanctuary. One of them said her father was coming to pick them up in about an hour. Perfect. The tour takes about an hour.

As I led them through the sanctuary, they were swept away. Happens every time. They fed raisins to Chester and Festus, laughed as Felipe leapt between branches, held Gomer close to their chests, and even sat down while Pablo and Coco, our mischievous white-faced capuchins, climbed into their laps and began grooming them like part of the troop.

The final stop, of course, was Bubba, our resident drama king. True to form, he put on his best "raccoon that's been bitten by a werewolf" routine, snarling and posturing like a wild beast… right before flopping over for a belly rub. He loved the spotlight.

Just as we wrapped up, a car pulled up at the gate. The girl's name was Nikki, and her father had arrived. He introduced himself as Tom. I took one look at him and immediately knew. This was a guy who had done things. Dressed casually, but with the quiet confidence of someone who had made his own way in life. He did not need to speak for me to know he had resources, and presence.

As his eyes scanned the sanctuary, I saw something light up. So I offered him a short tour. He accepted. We talked as we walked. That is when I learned Tom had just purchased Villas Alturas, one of the premier hotels near Dominical. I knew it well, a gorgeous hillside location, ocean views to die for, peaceful, tucked just far enough away from the highway to feel like a different world. I had stayed there before. I knew it had been for sale, but had not realized it had changed hands.

And then the conversation shifted. Tom turned to me, hands in his pockets, eyes focused. "You know, Mike, I'd love to have something like this at my hotel. How hard would it be to deal with the red tape from MINAE and set something like this up at Villas Alturas?" Inside me, fireworks went off. This could be it. But I kept it cool. Looked him square in the eye and I said: "Tom… you and I need to talk"

Chapter 22

Alturas Wildlife Sanctuary is Born

I was excited now no doubt about it but I was doing my best to keep a lid on it. When Tom looked me in the eye and said he wanted a sanctuary like this at his hotel, my mind immediately kicked into high gear. But all I said was, "Tom, Let's step into my office."

We sat down together at the little office table. A couple of cold beers were passed around, and as we settled in, something clicked. There was an instant connection between us two guys from the construction world, used to getting things done. I laid it all out for him: the sanctuary paperwork process in Costa Rica wasn't for the faint of heart. It was a slow, bureaucratic tangle of inspections, interviews, and waiting easily a year or more just to get the permits. And Tom? Well, Tom wasn't a man known for his patience. as I would come to understand. He leaned forward, looked me straight in the eye, and asked, "How do we get around it?"

That's when I decided to be completely honest. I told him about our struggles, the sabotage from the zip-line operators, the lack of access for tourists, and the steep, unforgiving road up Osa Mountain. I explained how we had been promised support and foot traffic from the other attractions on the mountain, but the promises had dried up. We had the animals. We had the mission. But we were suffocating financially.

Then I laid out the one viable alternative: move the existing sanctuary to his hotel property Villas Alturas. The animals, the permits, the experience, the team, we'd bring it all. Skip the red tape. Build faster. Do it right. He didn't hesitate. "How about this," he said. "Come with me now. Let's go see the site. If you think it'll work, we'll meet tomorrow and start working this out. We shook hands on it, and I jumped into the truck with him and the girls. I left Dannia in charge of the sanctuary she was more than capable and we headed down the mountain.

As we drove, I tried to recall everything I knew about Villas Alturas. It was a stunning property, perched just outside of Dominicalito less than mile from Dominical proper, where I'd started my journey years ago selling banana bread under a shade tree. On the beach. This was prime real estate: close to town, easy to access, with a steady flow of tourists from all over the world. That alone solved two of our biggest problems, location and accessibility.

When we arrived, Tom drove past the hotel's main parking lot and continued down a road I'd never been on. After about 200 yards We reached a gravel lot tucked out of sight. It was like opening a treasure chest. There were multiple buildings: one larger structure with two, ground floor apartments and an open-air patio upstairs with sweeping jungle views. Another small brick building had water, a sink, and even a refrigerator, perfect for food prep. A covered concrete slab nearby had washer and dryer hookups, gold in a sanctuary setting. And off to one side, there was a two-story building with a garage underneath and an air-conditioned apartment above. I immediately thought: clinic below, director's quarters above. It was shaping up nicely.

Then came the moment of truth we rounded the main structure to view the actual site Tom had in mind for the main part of the sanctuary. Where the permanent resident animals would be housed. What I saw almost brought tears to my eyes. A large, completely flat expanse stretched out before us about 150 feet long and 80 feet wide. To the left, the access road sloped gently down toward the hotel. To the right, the land dropped away gently, into forested hills with plenty of room for future expansion. And in the middle: a grassy, sunlit clearing, free of trees or shrubs.. i've been hoping for an area like this to implement an idea that had been cooking in my head for a long time.

I turned to Tom and gave him a slow, deliberate thumbs-up. "This'll work," I said "Better than I could've imagined." The plan was now in motion.

We agreed to meet the next morning at 10 a.m. to hash out the details. Tom took me back to Osa Mountain and Dannia was already waiting, practically vibrating with anticipation. When I told her what I'd seen, and what might be coming, we danced, literally danced through the rest of the afternoon feedings. We had dreamed of evolving the sanctuary into something bigger. Now it was within reach.

The next morning, we rose early, knocked out the cage cleaning and morning feeding, and handed the reins over to our most trusted volunteers. Dannia and I jumped into the truck and headed down the mountain to Villas Alturas, hearts pounding. Tom greeted us with a broad smile and strong coffee. We sat down, and within a couple of hours, the deal was done. Tom would form a new corporation to own the sanctuary. Dannia and I would each hold a 10% stake. Tom would cover the development costs. Dannia and I would bring the permits, experience, and most importantly the animals. The Osa Mountain sanctuary would be relocated. A new chapter was about to begin.

But one very big and very important final hurdle remained: MINAE approval. This is where Dannia shined. She was in the final stages of her law degree and had earned the respect of the MINAE officials over the years. She knew the system. She knew the people. And she knew how to get things done. We told her to make the call. While she worked the phones, Tom and I clinked beers and sketched out early ideas. Before long, Dannia returned with a grin that said everything we needed to know. "They'll be here tomorrow," she said. "10 a.m. On site." Bingo.

The next morning, we arrived early and shared nervous coffee under a palm tree. Right on time, two MINAE trucks pulled up. Five officials climbed out, three high ranking officials, I didn't know, two I did. As Dannia led the formal tour and explained the site, Tom and I hung back with the two officers I'd worked with many times before.

One of them leaned over and whispered to me, "We've had a lot of problems with the Osa Mountain people. Getting the sanctuary out of there, that's something we'll support if everything here looks good." Fifteen minutes later, Dannia returned with the others. All of them smiling. We had our approval. Not just permission, encouragement.

They told us to proceed with all due speed. Hugs were exchanged. Hands were shaken. Plans were made.

I turned to Tom and said, "It's going to be a pleasure doing business with you. But now I've got to get back to my animals and start drawing up the new sanctuary plans."

Alturas Wildlife Sanctuary was officially in progress.

The move that would save over 100 animals... had just begun.

Chapter 23

Construction and Conflict

As Dannia and I bumped down the winding jungle road from Osa Mountain, a storm of ideas swirled in my head like the rains of the green season. We had just secured the go-ahead for what felt like a miracle, the relocation and rebirth of our sanctuary at Villas Alturas. It was not just exciting, it was electrifying. For the first time in a long while, I felt hope turn into motion.

But even as optimism flooded my thoughts, caution crept alongside it. Dannia and I both knew that if word got out too soon, especially to the management at Osa Mountain, it would create waves. Possibly tidal waves. The politics on that mountain had already been turbulent, and we were now planning to relocate the sanctuary they once claimed as part of their draw. But the actual truth was the sanctuary that I had designed and built would still be theirs. All that was moving was Dannia and myself, our personal belongings, and the animals that I was the legal custodian of. We decided to keep the move quiet. For now, only a trusted few volunteer ladies would know. The animals came first. Their survival was not negotiable.

To manage both ends of the transition, Dannia would take a bigger leadership role at Osa Mountain while I made daily trips to Villas Alturas to oversee construction. That night, I did not sleep a wink. My mind raced with 1000 ideas of how to use the beautiful space we now had. By morning, I had sketched out a mental blueprint that excited me more than any project I had ever created.

At the heart of the new sanctuary, in that beautiful sunlit clearing, I envisioned a lush, elongated oval garden, roughly 70 feet long by 35 feet wide, ringed with a smooth, domed cinder block wall about five feet high. The curvature and finish were deliberate, no creature, no matter how clever, would be able to scale it. This would become a roaming paradise for our raccoons, coatis, tamanduas, and other ground dwellers who needed safety, stimulation, and space.

The garden's crown jewel was a 20-foot-diameter pond, deep enough to house tilapia, which would become an endless source of fascination for the resident raccoons.

Around the perimeter, I added naturalistic den sites, sewer pipes masked with rock work that blended beautifully into the jungle aesthetic. A couple of artfully placed dead trees in the middle of the enclosure gave the animals vertical real estate for climbing and surveying their kingdom. This was not just a holding pen, it was a jungle playground with purpose.

To the left of the garden, I designed a long row of smaller 6-by-4-foot cages, modular and versatile, perfect for medium-sized birds, mammals, or even reptiles. Across from them, larger enclosures for our monkeys and our not-so-cuddly Bubba. And at the far end, a grand parrot aviary purposely built as far away from the place where I would be sleeping as I could put it. This was a lesson I learned from experience. In the first sanctuary, parrots started screaming the minute the sun began to rise. Built for the lifers, these domesticated parrots, no longer wild by behavior or instinct, would have a spacious forever home filled with enrichment and attention. They could never be released. They would just fly to the nearest person and beg for crackers, which in Costa Rica can get you swatted with a broom.

As week one kicked off, we focused on gathering the materials. Cement, block, rebar, mesh, roofing, piles of it began appearing on-site. Tom wanted to use his own crew for the construction and insisted on paying by the hour. That was his first lesson in the "Tico Time" phenomenon. After three weeks, we had exactly one half of a cage built.

Tom was fuming. I stepped in. "Let me call my guys," I told him. These were the same men who helped me build my entire house in the jungle of Lagunas, a 4,000-square-foot fortress carved from sweat, concrete, and persistence. They did not waste time. They did not ask twice. They just built. Within two weeks of switching teams, the sanctuary was halfway done. Spirits lifted. Progress resumed.

Each day, I would start with a briefing at Osa Mountain, meet with Dannia, check the morning feedings, and then drive down one mountain and up the other to Villas Alturas. I would check progress, answer questions, solve problems, and coordinate schedules. Then I would head back for the afternoon routine and to care for the animals already under our protection. Life was good. For a moment. Then came the phone call.

Osa Mountain management had caught wind of our plan. They were livid. What followed was a predictable volley of threats and bluster. They claimed they would replace me. They threatened to take over the sanctuary themselves. What they did not understand, or chose not to understand, was that every single animal was bonded to me legally. MINAE had made that very clear. I was their guardian. And if I left, they left with me. I was not worried. I had MINAE's full support, and frankly, that trumped anything Osa Mountain had to say. Still, the hostility was a distraction, one more complication to navigate in a journey already paved with daily challenges. But I pressed on.

Finally, after weeks of cement, sweat, hauling, welding, trenching, wiring, roofing, and fencing, the day arrived. The cages stood ready. Electricity hummed. Plumbing flowed. The clinic was outfitted. The kitchen was prepped. And the apartment above the vet office, my new home, was waiting.The animals did not know it yet, but their new paradise was ready. It was time to move.

Chapter 24

Moving Day 1

The big day was finally here. This was it, the day we began moving approximately 100+ birds and animals from Osa Mountain to our new, improved, and much bigger sanctuary at Villas Alturas. And it was going to be a big job, too much for just Dannia and me, but I had already made the phone call, and help was on the way. At about 8:00 a.m., three MINAE trucks with six officers came rolling down the driveway, ready to help and to fend off any interference from the Osa Mountain management. Each truck had several animal crates in it, and we had about ten animal crates of various sizes at the sanctuary. Our new partner Tom had lent us a pickup truck from the hotel, and I would drive that.

I called everybody into the office, and we all sat down for a strategy meeting on how to begin this operation. It was decided that I would handle the animal and bird transfers, with the MINAE officers close by to assist when necessary. Dannia and the volunteer ladies would pack up as many of the baby and injured animals as we could manage on the first trip. It was obvious this complete move was going to require several trips.

I decided to start with the medium-sized mammals and wait on moving the parrots until all the mammals had been relocated. The first trip would include the creatures that were permanent sanctuary residents, animals that would never go back to the wild. This trip would include the mighty Bubba; Blossom the porcupine; Felipe the squirrel monkey and his three squirrel monkey friends; Lulu, the very young howler monkey who decided to cling to the back of my neck throughout the entire process; Pablo and Coco, the white-faced monkeys; Sweetie the kinkajou; Gomer the anteater; and Buster, a young coatimundi.

There was also Sophia the agouti, Tubby the paca, and many more. Meanwhile, Dannia had her hands full trying to corral four young four-eyed possums, as well as our young and very beautiful woolly opossum. The volunteer ladies were getting the small babies ready to go, which included a baby sloth named Nigel, a baby kinkajou named Casper, and three small raccoon kits that had been brought in after their mother was killed by a car. There were also many baby birds, mostly various parrot species, that had to be made ready to go on the first trip. The volunteer ladies would handle getting them ready.

Dannia and four of the MINAE officers would go with us on the first trip to Villas Alturas. She and two of the officers would stay behind at the new location to take care of the animals and get them into their designated cages or enclosures, while the rest of us returned for a second trip later that day and a third or possibly even a fourth trip the following day.

We concluded the meeting, and everyone got to work. By about 1:30 that afternoon, we were ready to roll. It was all very exciting. All the trucks were full of animals. I gave some final instructions to the volunteer ladies, and we mounted up and headed for Villas Alturas.

When we arrived, we found Tom and a couple of the hotel staff members waiting for us, eager to assist in any way necessary. We immediately pulled the trucks into the sanctuary and got to work. I discussed with Dannia and the two MINAE officials what animals were to go into what enclosure, then personally handled getting the mighty Bubba into his beautiful new enclosure first, mostly because everyone else was afraid of him.

That done, I, along with the two MINAE officers who were returning with me to Osa Mountain, jumped into the trucks and headed back for the next load of creatures, leaving Dannia to organize and try out our new, fully stocked kitchen to feed the animals that had just arrived at Villas Alturas.

As we headed back up the mountain road, I was both elated and energized by the success of the first trip and ready to start the second. Little did I know there was a situation waiting for me at the front gate of the sanctuary. As we rounded the corner onto the driveway, there stood two MINAE officers, members of Osa Mountain management, and two police officers from the town of Palmar Norte. The police officers and Osa Mountain management all had grim looks on their faces, but the MINAE officials were calm and smiling.

As I got out of the truck, one of the MINAE officials explained that the Osa Mountain management had called the police in an attempt to have Dannia and me escorted off the property to halt the moving of the animals. But the MINAE officials quickly explained to the police that the animals were legally bonded to me, that I was the legal custodian of every creature in the sanctuary, and that if I left, the animals had to leave with me. I was free to go, and no one could hold me there. As I have said before, MINAE trumps all other agencies in Costa Rica when it comes to matters involving wildlife or the environment. In other words, I was bulletproof.

With that settled, we got back to work preparing for the second trip of the day. The first order of business was the two big Geoffroy's spider monkeys, Chester and Festus. After my infamous cage match with Chester, we had grown to become friends, and I could now safely enter his cage. So I went in with a large dog crate, threw his favorite food, a big ripe mango, into the back of it, and he entered without a problem.

Now it was Festus's turn. Festus had a much different attitude, uncooperative and rebellious by nature. I could not blame him. Both monkeys had spent 20 years with collars around their necks, tied to a stick in someone's yard. But Festus had it even worse. At some point, someone had pulled all of his teeth. What I realized was that I was not getting him into a crate that day. I even tried tempting him with his favorite person, Dannia, but he would not go. After about an hour of trying, I gave up and moved Festus to the next day.

Next, I turned my attention to capturing and crating several parrots for the second trip. For this, I used one of the most effective tools a wildlife sanctuary has, the bath towel. For birds, a bath towel is incredibly useful. You drop it over them, and they immediately go still, allowing you to safely move them into a crate.

We had six large crates, four medium crates, and several smaller ones. Each large crate held two or three parrots depending on size. Medium crates held one large bird, and smaller crates held one medium-sized parrot. By late afternoon, we had the crates full with about one-third of our parrot population, along with Chester and other residents.

Our three-truck caravan slowly made its way down the mountain road. When we arrived at Villas Alturas, everything was ready. Dannia and the team had successfully placed every animal into its designated space.

While the birds were transferred into the aviary, I moved Chester into his new enclosure, a custom two-cage setup connected by a tunnel. Finally, the day's work was done. It was time for me to head back to Osa Mountain. The MINAE officials shook hands and told us they would not be returning the next day. They were confident we could handle the rest. It had been a great day. But tomorrow was another day.

<h1 style="text-align:center">Chapter 25</h1>

<h1 style="text-align:center">Moving Day 2</h1>

When I arrived back at Osa Mountain that evening, the first thing I did was call a friend who owned a large box truck. I arranged for him to arrive first thing in the morning to move my belongings and the remaining sanctuary equipment.

Right on time, he showed up with two helpers and got to work. I had already packed most of my things, and there was not much furniture. While they loaded the truck, I continued catching and crating the remaining parrots.

By the time I finished loading my truck, I realized there would only be one final trip after this. The box truck was already full with my belongings and the portable cages I had built years earlier in Lagunas. We headed for Villas Alturas.

When we arrived, everything was running smoothly. The animals were settled, and the sanctuary looked incredible. We unloaded the birds into the aviary, then headed back for the final trip. At Osa, the movers loaded the remaining equipment while I gathered the last parrots.

Then it was time for Festus. As I entered the cage with the crate, he watched me closely. He seemed to understand something was happening. He had not seen Chester since the day before. I opened the crate, placed a banana inside, and waited. He walked in. No fight. No resistance. I loaded him into the truck and took one final look around the sanctuary. It was time.

When we arrived at Villas Alturas, the first priority was reuniting Chester and Festus. As soon as I opened the crate, Chester began calling out. Festus responded immediately. Their excitement was undeniable. We placed Festus into the adjacent enclosure and opened the connecting doors.

They rushed toward each other and embraced, wrapping arms and tails together in a moment of pure recognition and relief. It was one of the most powerful moments I had ever witnessed. Once they settled in, we finished moving the remaining parrots. And just like that, it was done.

We walked through the sanctuary, checking every enclosure. Everything was working. Everything felt right. Finally, I went up to my new apartment above the clinic and looked around. This was home. That evening, Dannia and I met Tom for dinner.

In three days, we would open the sanctuary to the public.

Chapter 26

Getting Ready to Open

The sanctuary was buzzing with life, not just from the animals, but from the anticipation. We were officially opening the doors in three days, on Sunday, and there was still a mountain of work to be done before then. But after what we had just been through, the move, the chaos, the emotion, this felt like the beginning of something truly extraordinary. Tom, Dannia, and I decided to host a proper opening ceremony, something that honored the journey and the people who had helped us along the way. We agreed to invite the MINAE officials who had approved the sanctuary, along with the local business owners and hotel operators, many of whom already knew what we were building at Villas Alturas.

Dominical is a small town, and news travels like wildfire, especially when animals and something new are involved. Still, we wanted to make it official. So we planned a gathering on the upstairs deck overlooking the entire sanctuary. At 1:00 p.m. Sunday, we would kick things off with a short welcome speech, then open the gates for a first walk-through. It was important that the community feel included. This sanctuary was not mine, or Tom's, or Dannia's. It was for the animals and, by extension, for the community that would help sustain them. I took on the task of personally inviting every hotel and business owner I knew, and I knew a lot of them. Years of baking and selling banana bread on the beach, and years of organizing local spay and neuter clinics for dogs, had connected me to just about everyone who mattered in Dominical. This was not about blasting social media or running ads. This was about face-to-face contact and real community. At the same time, Tom and I had a deeper conversation about one of the most important things we would need to sustain the sanctuary long-term, a volunteer program. I explained that volunteers were not just helpful, they were essential. There is no shortage of work at a sanctuary. Every day it is cleaning, feeding, repairing, moving, checking, and watching. Tom, ever the savvy businessman, immediately understood the value. Not only could a volunteer program help cover our labor needs, it could also generate income.

Without hesitation, he pledged to build a four-bedroom volunteer house, with two bunks per room to house up to eight volunteers at a time. He also committed to creating a website where people from all over the world could apply to come help and experience the jungle firsthand, for a price.

Meanwhile, Dannia headed off to the nearby towns on dual missions. First, she contacted our trusted local veterinarian to ask about any vets who might be available to work at the new sanctuary. Second, she traveled to San Isidro to order a batch of promotional flyers to distribute in Dominical and the surrounding areas. By Sunday morning, the whole town was talking. People were calling the hotel, emailing, and even stopping by in person to reserve spots for upcoming tours. Word had definitely gotten out. We had also decided that once the sanctuary opened to the public, we would close every Monday for deep cleaning and catch-up.

Tuesday through Sunday would be for tours, with me, of course, as the guide.

The upstairs deck was looking great. Dannia and some of the hotel staff had set up a small bar, arranged seating, and made everything feel festive but still grounded in the mission. The view from up there was incredible. On one side, you could see the full sanctuary, the enclosures, the garden, the aviary, the energy of life. On the other, you saw the clinic, the intake area, and the quiet section designated for animals being prepped for release, those that needed isolation and minimal human contact. It was the full picture, both the care and the hope.

By noon, people were already gathering. By 1:00 p.m., the deck was full, nearly thirty people, all curious and excited to see what we had created. Eagerly peering from the deck down into the garden, Tom, Dannia, and I stood side by side as we gave short speeches. We thanked everyone for coming. We thanked MINAE for their partnership. We spoke from the heart about the purpose of the sanctuary, and how it would now be open to the public, not just for viewing, but for learning and, hopefully, for inspiring. Then we invited everyone to descend the staircase and enter the sanctuary.I had the privilege of leading the very first official tour of Alturas Wildlife Sanctuary that day.

As I walked our guests through the cages, the garden, and the trees, I told the story of every single animal. I knew them all. Their names. Their injuries. Their personalities. Their triumphs. Because they were not just animals, they were survivors. As the sun began to sink, people started drifting back up toward the hotel and the bar. Some lingered, others departed. The sanctuary slowly quieted. And while others celebrated, Dannia, a few volunteers, and I turned back toward the animals.We still had mouths to feed. Because that is the truth about running a sanctuary: the celebration might end, but the work never does.

Chapter 27

The First Tours Begin

By Tuesday morning, everything was in place. The sanctuary
gleamed with promise, the animals were settled in, and I stood
at the edge of something we had dreamed about for years.
Dannia had just returned from San Isidro, her arms full of
freshly printed flyers, and with them, a surprise that made
everyone stop in admiration. At the center of each flyer was a
stunning circular logo she had designed herself: a silhouette of
a monkey swinging wild and free, with the words "Rescue.
Rehab. Release." curved underneath. It was bold. It was
beautiful. And it perfectly captured who we were. I took one
look and said, "That's it. Put that on T-shirts. Put it on
everything." It was not just a slogan. It was our mission.

Monday was our last full prep day before opening. I spent
it pacing the grounds and rehearsing. I had done plenty of
tours at the Osa sanctuary, but this was different. This was
official. Three tours a day, 10:00 a.m., 12:00 p.m., and 2:00
p.m., six days a week, with Mondays reserved for deep
cleaning. I calculated each tour would run an hour to an hour
and a half, maybe a little more if the questions kept coming,
and I hoped they would. When Tuesday morning came, I was
ready. We had about 15 to 20 people booked for each of the

day's three tours. I stood near the sanctuary gate, nervously scanning the path that led from the hotel.

Then I saw them, the first tour group walking down the road toward me. A mix of tourists and familiar faces from my days selling banana bread on the beach in Dominical. As they arrived, I realized I was not the only one excited. These folks were buzzing with curiosity and anticipation. I welcomed them in, and the first official tour of the Alturas Wildlife Sanctuary began. As we wound through the sanctuary paths, I shared the stories of our residents, some heartwarming, others heartbreaking, but all true. I told them about Bubba, our mighty coati. About Blossom the porcupine and Pablo the monkey. I spoke about Nigel the baby sloth, and Tommy the raccoon with crippled legs who never knew he was handicapped. These were not exhibits. These were lives. Stories of survival. Of second chances. And I told every one of them to emphasize the most important truth of all: wild animals do not make good pets.

Per MINAE rules, the tour stayed within the public sanctuary zone. The veterinary clinic, nursery, and release zones remained off-limits. But we knew what people wanted to see most: baby animals. So we would bring them out carefully, just for a moment, so guests could snap a photo and feel the joy of seeing something so innocent and rare. Day after day, the tours grew more popular. We capped each at 20 people, and every slot began to fill. On TripAdvisor, we climbed fast, from somewhere down the list to one of the top-rated things to do in all of Costa Rica. Five-star reviews poured in, praising the experience, the mission, and yes, even the tour guide. Financially, it was the breakthrough we needed. The tours brought in hundreds of dollars a day, and our eight-bed volunteer house filled quickly, solving our labor problem while boosting the sanctuary income even more. But two critical pieces were still missing: we needed a veterinarian, and we needed a biologist. I had already reached out to Larissa, a brilliant biologist from Brazil I had met during her volunteer stint at Osa. She was sharp, compassionate, fluent in English, and most importantly, she got it. She understood what we were trying to do. Three days after opening, we received her reply. She was coming in four days. It was the best news we could have hoped for. That just left one last piece of the puzzle: a veterinarian. Dannia had already spread the word far and wide, and I had no doubt that someone would step forward soon. In the meantime, we had work to do. The gates of the new sanctuary had officially opened, and the world was starting to notice.

Chapter 28

New Arrivals

The moment the sanctuary gates officially opened to the public, the real work began. Just as expected, and a bit sooner than we were ready for, the MINAE trucks started showing up.

The first few arrivals were nothing we had not seen before. Three Red-lored Amazon parrots, two more baby raccoons, and a pair of young chestnut-mandible toucans that had fallen from their nest, strikingly similar to Heckle and Jekyll from my early days in Lagunas. By the end of the week, our veterinarian problem had a temporary fix. A young guy named Pablo, visiting from Spain, was in the area for a couple of months. He was not a long-term solution, but his enthusiasm made up for that. He was thrilled to jump in, and we were just as thrilled to have the pressure off, even for a little while.

Midway through week two, everything was humming. The volunteer effort was becoming dialed in, the animals were fed and cared for, and the tours were booking up like we had hoped. Then I got the text I had been waiting for. "Hi Mike, I'm in Dominical. Can you come pick me up?" It was Larissa.

Larissa was a biologist I had met back at Osa Mountain when she came to volunteer. Brazilian, smart, caring, fluent in English, and absolutely dedicated to wildlife. When we opened

113

the new sanctuary, I had reached out and offered her a job on the spot. Now, here she was.

Ten minutes later, I pulled up to the bus stop in Dominical. She stood there with all her bags and that unmistakable smile, the kind of smile that told me this was going to work. We hugged, loaded her stuff into the truck, and headed up the road toward Villas Alturas.

Her new home was the apartment inside the central sanctuary building, a simple place, but it had a fridge, a bed, and a roof. That is all anyone working at a wildlife sanctuary really needs. Once she settled in, I gave her a whirlwind tour of the grounds. She lit up like a kid at Christmas. Then it was up to the restaurant for food, drinks, and introductions to Tom. By the time we rolled back down the hill, the three of us were buzzing with excitement about what the next day would bring. And it came early.

At 5:30 a.m., I was up with a cup of coffee, and by 6:00 I was in the prep kitchen with Dannia, Larissa, and three of our best volunteers to kick off morning feeding. But before we could even chop the first papaya, my phone rang. A woman out walking her dog near a coastal community about 20 miles south had spotted something unusual. A baby three-toed sloth alone on the ground.

Now, here is the thing about sloths. If a baby falls from its mother, she often will not come down to get it. It is just not in their nature. And on the jungle floor, a baby sloth is vulnerable, especially if nobody notices. This one got lucky. I did not say a word. I just told the team I would be back in an hour, jumped in my truck, and hit the road.

When I pulled up, the woman was waiting, cradling a small box. Inside, wrapped in cloth, was one of the most beautiful baby three-toed sloths I had ever seen, a young female, maybe a month old at most. Her soft face peeked out from under the cloth, blinking at the daylight, lost but curious. I thanked the woman for her kindness and made the drive back with my tiny passenger nestled beside me.

Back at the sanctuary, Dannia and Larissa were already outside, waiting like they knew something was up. Dannia's instincts were razor sharp when it came to me disappearing in a hurry. I walked up, lifted the box, and said to Larissa, "Here's your first baby." She beamed. She did not need instructions. She whisked the baby sloth away to the nursery, prepared the goat milk, and started the hydration protocol. This baby, soon named Bonita, was in good hands.

Sloths were not something we got many of at Osa. In all our time there, I think we only took in one. But here at Alturas, they were common. Very common. And we were quickly discovering that baby sloths were a whole different game. Why? Because raising one in captivity means it probably cannot go back to the wild. The feeding behaviors and forest skills a young sloth needs to survive have to be taught by its mother. Without her, the sloth will never thrive alone. That meant we were going to be keeping most of the sloths that arrived. So we got to work designing dedicated enclosures, circular garden-style spaces about 20 feet across, with big central climbing structures and low-impact landscaping. It needed to be safe, natural, and immersive, for them and for our visitors. And oh boy, the visitors. If you thought people loved monkeys, wait until they see a baby sloth. Tour guests melted into puddles of awe-struck mush. They loved Bonita. It was impossible not to.

Larissa took her surrogate role so seriously it was hard not to smile. She carried Bonita everywhere in a handmade sling, just like a mother sloth would. Bonita clung to her and watched the world go by with slow, blinking wonder. Within weeks, Alturas Wildlife Sanctuary was fully alive. The tours were popular. The animals were thriving. New arrivals came in steadily. And somehow, everything was working.

For now.

Chapter 29

More New Arrivals and Trouble in Paradise

By the third week, the rhythm of sanctuary life was in full swing, and so were the new arrivals. That was when MINAE brought us a beautiful adult three-toed sloth. The poor thing had been the victim of a power line incident, a sadly common hazard in this part of Costa Rica. But as much as we wanted to care for it ourselves, the timing was not right. We simply were not yet equipped to house an adult sloth in a proper enclosure. Keeping it cooped up in a dog crate did not sit right with us.

So we decided to transfer the sloth to a place that was world-renowned for its work, the Sloth Sanctuary on the Caribbean coast, just south of Limón. It was the right decision for the animal's well-being. But in Costa Rica, even the right decision has to be backed by paperwork.

MINAE has very strict protocols. Any transport of a wild animal, especially one crossing the country, requires formal authorization. The paperwork must list the specific individual who will be doing the transport by name. No exceptions.

The sloth had arrived late in the day, and we were all gathered in the staging area, Dannia, Larissa, Tom, and me. As we discussed our plan to head to the MINAE office in Palmar

Norte the next morning to get the paperwork, Tom started pacing. Then it happened.

Tom exploded. He did not just disagree with the plan, he detonated. He wanted to send the sloth out that night with a hotel employee so no sanctuary staff had to leave the grounds. When we told him that was not allowed, he completely lost it. He screamed about how stupid the MINAE rules were, and he did so loudly, directly in front of the MINAE officers who had just delivered the sloth. We were stunned.

Until that moment, Tom had always come across as practical, smart, and supportive. But now he was standing red-faced in front of government wildlife officials, shouting about how ridiculous their regulations were, the same regulations we depended on to operate. To make matters worse, one of the MINAE officers was on the phone with headquarters. Meaning Tom's tirade was not just for the field agents. It was being broadcast directly to the upper chain of command. Dannia, Larissa, and I looked at each other, cringing.

Dannia jumped in to defuse the situation, grabbed the officer's phone, and calmly explained that we understood the rules, that this was a misunderstanding, and that we would handle things appropriately. Meanwhile, I pulled Tom aside and did my best to calm him down. It was not easy. Eventually, we came to a compromise. I would immediately drive the 30 miles to Palmar Norte to get the paperwork before the office closed. Once I returned, Tom's hotel employee could make the overnight drive to the Sloth Sanctuary legally.

I jumped in my truck and headed south, knowing full well I would be walking into a scolding. And sure enough, when I arrived at the MINAE office, the officers did not hold back. They made it crystal clear that Tom's outburst had insulted the very people we needed to survive. They warned me that if it continued, it could jeopardize everything.I took it on the chin. Back at Alturas, Dannia and Larissa had the sloth prepared and ready. I handed off the paperwork, and we sent the animal on its way, safely, legally, and properly.

As the weeks passed, a new rhythm settled in. Early morning cleaning. Morning feeding. Three guided tours a day. Afternoon feedings. Animal intakes. Animal releases. Each day brought more arrivals and the occasional goodbye. And those goodbyes were the best part of all.

Releasing an animal back to the wild was the most rewarding thing we did. But it required planning. We always wanted to know where an animal had originally been found. Releasing it back into its home territory gave it the best chance at survival, where it knew the food and water sources and the lay of the land.

One of my favorite release stories involved a spectacular and perplexing guest, a full-grown spectacled owl. Someone had found it on the ground, looking dazed. When we took it in, it quickly became apparent that something was very wrong. It would sit on a perch with its head completely upside down, the top of its head pointing straight at the floor. It was unsettling. Any time it tried to move, it would tumble off the perch and flop awkwardly around.

We examined it carefully. No broken bones. No injuries. No physical trauma. Just this bizarre, inverted posture. We were stumped. Then one of the visiting biologists suggested something we had not considered, an inner ear issue. Possibly mites. We began treatment immediately. Slowly, day by day, the owl began to straighten up. Literally. Over the course of a few weeks, the head tilt diminished, the balance returned, and the owl started perching like a normal bird again. It was subtle progress at first, but unmistakable.

Then one evening at dusk, Larissa and I took him to the edge of the mountains where he had originally been found. We opened the crate, and he stepped out tentatively, then launched into the trees, gliding away on those powerful wings like he had never been grounded. It was beautiful.

As I stood there watching him disappear into the canopy, I could not help but think once again, this is why we do this.

Chapter 30

Escapes and Losses

Running a wildlife sanctuary with scores of different exotic species is difficult at best. To do it perfectly is impossible. There will always be losses and occasional escapes. Many of the animals that come in have been fatally injured before they ever arrive.

After the second week, we started to notice troubling signs coming from Gomer and Buster, our young coatis. This concerned me greatly, and I began to watch them closely. A couple of days later, I saw Gomer suddenly stiffen up and have a full-blown seizure. I immediately scooped him up and got him to the vet. Slowly, he came out of it and seemed okay for the moment. The day after that, we found Buster lying on the ground, apparently unable to move.

We immediately got them both to the vet, along with our veterinarian Pablo, and they began working on them. The diagnosis came back: they had been exposed to something toxic. It turned out that one of the decorative plants in the garden was highly toxic, and none of us knew it.

The vets worked very hard to save both animals. Pablo was communicating with his contacts all over the world, trying to find an antidote to the toxins that had gotten into Gomer and

Buster, but to no avail. We lost both of them. It was heartbreaking, especially the loss of Gomer, who had been with me for more than two years.

As time went on at Alturas Wildlife Sanctuary, everything seemed to operate smoothly. For the first time, I felt like I could actually start to take one day a week off. I had not had a day off since I started the Osa sanctuary more than three years earlier.

It seemed like Mondays would be the natural day off for me. The sanctuary was closed, there were no tours, and Dannia, the volunteers, and the staff were conducting deep cleaning. So Mondays became the day I would go to the nearby town of San Isidro to pay my bills, handle my banking, and do whatever shopping I needed to do.

On one particularly beautiful Monday afternoon, I was heading back to the sanctuary from San Isidro when my phone rang. It was Tom, screaming as usual. I was beginning to understand that this was Tom's normal state of being. What he was screaming about was that one of the volunteers had allowed Chester and Festus to escape. Festus was in the top of one of the tall trees next to the sanctuary, but Chester had made his way up to the hotel restaurant and caused a mess, throwing a guest's lunch around the restaurant and biting somebody's dog.

I told Tom to calm down, that I was about ten minutes away and would be there as quickly as possible to resolve the issue. I did not know how I was going to resolve it, but that is what I told him. I made the turn onto the sanctuary road, sped up the half-mile mountain road as fast as I could, passed the hotel, and was just about to turn into the driveway of the staging area. As I crested the small hill, there he was, standing in the road, Chester, the escapee.

Obviously, he had left the restaurant and made his way back down to the sanctuary. Dannia was there about 50 feet behind him, just following him around and monitoring his activity. Chester had heard and recognized the sound of my truck coming up the hill and turned to meet me. When I saw him, I stopped immediately, and so did he.

I got out of the truck, spread my arms, and said, "Come here, Chester." He started walking toward me. That was when it all went sideways. Standing just off to the side of the road was Romero, the hotel gardener and groundskeeper. He was quietly watching what was happening and not moving. He was wearing black rubber boots that went up to just below his knees, standard Tico gear that every Costa Rican working outside wears.

As Chester got closer to me, he noticed Romero standing there and instantly changed course. He went straight for Romero, jumped on his leg, wrapped himself around it, and started ripping at the boot with his teeth, actually biting chunks out of the rubber. The situation had instantly turned from manageable to very serious.

I give Romero credit for not panicking. He reached down and tried to pull Chester off his leg. By that time, I was already there, trying to help him. But a grown Geoffroy's spider monkey is as strong as a man. Our efforts were having no effect. Romero had managed to grab the back of Chester's head and was pushing it against his leg in a way that stopped him from biting. But now he was trapped. He could not let go, and Chester was not letting go either.

At that point, I was getting very worried about what would happen next. Romero was bleeding enough to be concerning, Chester was still fighting and trying to bite, and in his other hand Romero was holding a machete. If the situation got any worse, he might use it.

There had been an incident back at Osa about a year and a half earlier where a government biologist had accidentally let Chester escape. In that instance, I had been able to walk up to him, take my belt off, slip it around his waist, and thread it through the buckle. As soon as I did that, Chester was happy to walk like a well-trained little puppy right back into his cage. I attributed this to the fact that Chester had spent 19 years tied to a stake in someone's yard before the government brought him to me. I also believed that his attack on Romero's rubber boots was likely a trauma response, probably the result of some abuse involving rubber boots that he experienced while tied to that stake. But right then, that belt move was my only option. If it did not work, Romero might think he had no other choice but to use that machete.

I pulled off my belt, slipped it around Chester's waist, threaded it back through the buckle, and stepped back. I had no idea what was going to happen next. Chester might come off. He might not. He might come off in a rage and attack me, or not. Here we go. I did not yank. I just put tension on the belt and started to pull. Then something amazing happened. Chester immediately let go of Romero's leg, and I found myself holding the belt at arm's length with Chester suspended in the air on the end of it, completely calm and not attacking me. Thank God.

It could have gotten very ugly. I could have ended up in another fight with Chester. Romero, with his hand bleeding profusely, immediately headed down the hill and back to the hotel for first aid. Dannia and I headed through the staging area with Chester calmly walking at my side toward the monkey cage, Dannia walking ahead of me to open the door. I led Chester inside.

That only left the ever-obstinate and uncooperative Festus to be captured. He was sitting in the top of a tall tree next to the sanctuary gate. The only option was to wait for him to come down, then somehow try to grab him. The worry was that he would move off into the jungle.

Now, Festus could be grabbed because he did not have any teeth, so he could not bite. But he could scream, scratch, and slap. And he would do all three when grabbed. Even though he had no teeth to sink into you, it could be very intimidating when he started to go crazy. So the move was to sit at the base of the tree and wait for him to get hungry enough to come down. There was no way he was going to come to me. He knew very well that if he did, he would be grabbed and returned to his cage. But it was a different matter for Larissa. Festus loved Larissa. So she was stationed at the bottom of the tree with a banana and a mango to wait. Meanwhile, the afternoon feeding was happening in the sanctuary right below the tree where he was sitting, and he could see it all. We knew he had to be getting hungry. So we sat and waited, Larissa at the bottom of the tree while I sat about 50 yards away on a rock, ready to help when needed.

After about two hours, Festus started to descend from the top of the tree down toward Larissa. I watched tensely as she held out a banana. As Festus reached for it, she snatched him by the hand.

I will say this, I was impressed by Larissa's courage. Even knowing Festus could not bite, grabbing him was no small thing. The rage he exhibited when grabbed was very intimidating indeed. I immediately got to my feet and ran over as fast as I could. By then, she had him by both hands. I grabbed him by both feet, and together we carried the screaming, struggling Festus back to his cage and gently put him in, where he and Chester immediately wrapped their arms around each other and chittered up a storm, telling each other about the adventures they had that day.

Chapter 31

New Problems, New Opportunities

As time went on at Alturas, we dialed in our procedures and systems until everything was running very efficiently. We had finally secured a permanent veterinarian, a lady named Laura, and we had a volunteer coordinator whose job was to help our volunteers stay busy, focused, and entertained. The volunteers' main functions were cage cleaning, moving food from the kitchen to the enclosures under Dannia's direction, and small construction projects under mine. Dannia was in charge of feeding and knew every animal's dietary requirements. We fed twice a day, which kept her busy.

About 80 percent of my time was spent giving tours, with the other 20 percent spent signing in new animals and performing whatever other tasks were necessary to keep the sanctuary running smoothly. As the weeks turned into months, and then into our second year, everything was going like clockwork, except for one glitch: Tom.

Tom was not a happy guy. Whenever something went wrong with hotel operations or in his personal life, he would come down to the animal sanctuary and start yelling and screaming, as if determined to make everybody as miserable as he was. Over time, his behavior caused problems with MINAE. He complained constantly about their rules and regulations.

But he also created tension with the volunteers, with the staff, and with me. His complaints were never actually about the sanctuary, nor should they have been, because the sanctuary was running perfectly. His rants stemmed from his own frustrations, and we were all stuck hearing about them.

Early in our third year, I received a message from the MINAE office. The regional director, a man named Nelson, had requested a meeting with me. He asked if I could come to the MINAE office in San Isidro the following day. I agreed, curious, because when a regional director wants to talk, it is guaranteed to be important.

I arrived at his office around 10:00 a.m. We exchanged greetings and sat down, and Nelson got right to the point. He explained that he was concerned about another sanctuary in his jurisdiction, the IRescue Wildlife Sanctuary, located about three and a half hours from Alturas, deep in the cloud forests of the country's central mountains. The owner, a man named John, had been issued permits to open the sanctuary and had taken in many birds and some animals. But then, for reasons unknown, he made a trip to Colombia and became stranded there due to a passport issue. He was not expected to return to Costa Rica for six months to a year.

I was already acquainted with John. In fact, over the last couple of years, I had moved animals from Alturas up to his sanctuary. It was a beautiful place, 500 hectares of primary rainforest in the mountains.

There were two buildings on the property: the main house that John had built for himself, and a smaller Tico-style house he had stayed in while building the main house. There were also two geodesic domes built for birds and several small animal enclosures scattered around the property. Currently, three Tico workers were coming in daily to care for the animals, but they were not trained or qualified for that kind of work.

Nelson had already spoken to John, and between the two of them they had come up with a proposal. Would I be willing to go rescue the IRescue sanctuary and leave Dannia as director of Alturas? By the time he finished explaining this idea, my head was spinning. On the one hand, I did not want to leave Alturas. I had conceived, designed, created, and nurtured this sanctuary into being. It was doing exactly what I had dreamed: returning animals to the wild, healing the injured, and giving the abused a safe new life. In other words, I had built my dream, and it was working.

On the other hand, there were now animals in need. A population at risk. And I was being offered a chance to do it all again on a new blank slate, in an entirely different part of the country, high in the magical cloud forests of Costa Rica. It was exciting. Tempting. The bugs had all been worked out at Alturas. The place ran itself. Dannia was more than capable of taking over as director and tour guide.

After the meeting, I shook Nelson's hand and told him I was intrigued but needed a few days to think it over. There were going to be complications. First, there was the issue of custody of the animals. But Nelson said that was not a problem. He could reassign custodial responsibility to Dannia if she agreed to take over as director. The bigger issue was going to be Tom.

When I got back to Alturas, I did not tell Dannia about the meeting, not yet. Instead, I asked her to do something I had been meaning to ask for a while. "Can you check on the corporation documents for Alturas Wildlife Sanctuary?" When we had made the original deal with Tom, it was agreed that he would be 80 percent owner, and Dannia and I would each be 10 percent owners. We had shaken hands on it, so I had assumed that was the way he had set it up. But when Dannia came back to me with her findings, I was shocked. Tom had not honored the deal at all. He had made himself 100 percent owner of the corporation. Dannia and I owned nothing. For some reason, Dannia did not seem too upset by this revelation, but I definitely was.

I marched up to the hotel, found Tom in his office, shut the door, and asked him point-blank, "Why didn't you honor the deal we made?" He smirked, shrugged, and said, "It is what it is." At that moment, something clicked inside me. The universe was pointing me toward a new direction. I resisted the urge to reach across the desk and choke Tom out. Instead, I got up calmly, walked out of the office, proud of myself for resisting the overpowering urge for violence, and headed down to talk to Dannia. She saw the look on my face and immediately knew something serious had happened. "I didn't strangle him," I said. "But I thought about it."

Then I told her about the meeting with Nelson and the urgent need for help at IRescue. I explained that when I first got back, I was not sure what to do. But after my conversation with Tom, I was now seriously considering it. Still, I said I would talk to Tom one more time before deciding. Maybe, just maybe, he would reconsider.

The next morning, I gathered my thoughts, calmed my nerves, and headed back to the hotel. Tom was sitting at a table in the restaurant, drinking coffee and reading paperwork. I walked over, sat down, and told him, "If you're not going to honor our original deal, I'm considering leaving the sanctuary." He laughed directly in my face "You're not going anywhere." At that moment, I considered violence again. But instead, I walked out, again.

Back at the sanctuary, Dannia was waiting, clearly concerned. I told her what had happened. And I told her, "I'm taking the job at IRescue. And you're going to be the new director of Alturas." It was an emotional moment. But I knew Dannia could handle it. And if I stayed, the situation with Tom would only escalate. It was sad to leave. But in the back of my mind, there was that familiar spark. That old feeling in the pit of my stomach. That feeling that meant a new adventure was beginning.

Chapter 32

New Horizons and New Challenges

My mind was spinning. The recent chain of events had made one thing clear: the universe was pointing me to IRescue. There were birds and animals up there that needed help. But before I made my final decision, I planned to take a trip to the IRescue Sanctuary in two days, on Monday, my day off, to check out the situation firsthand. I decided to avoid speaking with Tom until after that visit.

Later that evening, I got a call from Colombia. It was John, the owner of IRescue. Apparently, he had spoken to Nelson after our meeting, and Nelson had told him that I had not said no and that I was seriously considering taking over as director.

John was in his late 30s, a wealthy businessman who was currently stuck in Colombia for reasons he did not explain. He told me it would be a minimum of six months before he could return to Costa Rica, possibly longer, but he wanted me to stay on even if and when he returned. I told him I would be heading up to the sanctuary Monday to evaluate the situation. He said he would notify his workers so they could show me around. He was very worried about the birds and animals already there and was doing his best to persuade me to take the job. He even offered me my choice of either of the two houses on the property to live in.

Sunday came and went with only one incident of note: two hotel staff members came down to the sanctuary, visibly disturbed. They said Tom was fighting with his girlfriend and throwing a tantrum in the hotel lobby. Standing there listening to them describe the scene, I thought again to myself that, as much as I regretted it, I was going to have to leave Alturas. I was finding it harder every day to tolerate Tom.

Monday morning arrived, and I hopped into my truck to begin the three-and-a-half-hour drive to the IRescue Sanctuary, located high in the mountains above the town of Pejibaye in central Costa Rica. To get to John's property, I passed through town and turned onto the road leading up the mountain. The road was every bit as rugged as the road to Osa, and twice as long. At Osa, the bad road had been a problem because it affected our ability to finance the sanctuary through tourism. But here, that would not be an issue. This sanctuary was funded by John and his donors, not by public tours.

As I climbed higher, the foliage began to change. I was now higher in the Costa Rican mountains than I had ever been before. The weather was perfect, a huge relief from the sweltering temperatures at Alturas. When I finally arrived at the first gate to John's property, it was easy to see why this was called the cloud forest. There were huge tracts of primary forest all around, separated by patches of open pasture. Even at midday, low-hanging clouds drifted through the trees.

The first gate opened into a large pasture filled with impressive Brahman cattle. I went through, closed the gate behind me, and continued through the pasture until I reached the second gate, the one that opened to the sanctuary grounds and the houses.

As I rounded a small curve and crested a hill, I found myself on a wide, flat plateau. To my left was a large open space, bigger than the entire sanctuary at Alturas. To my right was a small Tico-style house with a fenced yard. I immediately noticed avocado and mandarin trees growing there. Nice.

Waiting for me were John's three Tico workers: Juan, the farm manager, and his helpers, Josué and Taco. Together, these three men managed the property and were doing their best to care for the animals. But managing land that big in the jungle is a lot of work. Just keeping the jungle cut back is a full-time job. Add animal care on top, and they were stretched thin. They were happy to see me. We exchanged greetings. Juan spoke pretty good English, and it was clear we would be able to communicate well enough to get things done.

We started by checking out the small house. It was a modest one-bedroom, one-bathroom home with a living room and kitchen. John had lived there while building the big house and had remodeled it. It was actually very nice inside, with all the necessary appliances, water, and electricity. Then Juan led me up to the big house on the hill, because John had told him that was where I would be staying. This house was incredible. It was more of a lodge than a home. John had flown in a large log cabin kit and a construction crew from the U.S. to assemble it. It sat high on the hill, with sweeping views in every direction. Beautiful appliances, furniture, and a big-screen TV. Even an $8,000 couch. It was way more house than I needed or wanted. I told Juan that John had said I could choose where to live, and if that was true, I would be taking the Tico house at the bottom of the hill.

Next, we checked on the animals and birds. There were two large geodesic domes. In one dome was a single osprey who had been blinded in one eye and could not be released. The second dome was jammed full of Amazon parrots, several different types, along with smaller parrots and a flock of tiny orange-chinned parakeets, pericos, all housed together. This was a bad situation for many reasons, and it would be the first thing I would fix if I came on board.

We walked past a few small wooden cages, most of them already starting to rot. One held an owl with one wing. Another held four baby raccoons suffering from malnutrition-induced blindness and poorly developed fur. I had seen this before. Their diet lacked protein, causing their eyes to cloud and their coats not to develop. I knew the solution. "Put them on a strict diet of fish only, immediately," I told Juan.

Then we walked to a large fenced area, maybe an acre in size, where two Costa Rican white-tailed deer lived. Both were adults. Neither could be released. They had no fear of humans or dogs, which would be a death sentence in the wild. Suddenly, I heard the fluttering of wings, and right in front of us landed an old friend. Harpo.

Harpo was a crested guan, a jungle bird about the size of a turkey. He had come to us at Osa as a tiny chick. We raised him to adulthood and gave him full freedom to live around the sanctuary uncaged, and he stayed. But as an adult, Harpo developed a strange quirk. He was completely intolerant of human females. He would immediately attack any woman he saw, running at them, flapping his wings, and kicking with his claws. It got so bad that we had to take his freedom and cage him. He hated it. He was not meant for captivity. That was when I called John and asked if I could move Harpo up to his place, where there were no women there.

Since then, Harpo had bonded with the three Ticos and followed them everywhere like a domesticated poodle. When he saw me with them, he flew down and greeted me with a series of excited squawks. He recognized me, even after all that time. Another sign?

By then, I had seen what I needed to see. My mind was pretty much made up. I gave Juan final instructions for the raccoons and parrots, shook each of their hands, and told them I would likely be seeing them again very soon. Then I got back on the road toward Alturas.

Since it was still early afternoon, I decided to swing through San Isidro and stop at the MINAE office to let Nelson know I had decided to take the job, but that I wanted to work out a few details first. I wanted Nelson to officially enforce the change of directorship at Alturas, switching it from me to Dannia and no one else, and make it so that Tom could not interfere. I also wanted to be able to transfer certain animals from Alturas to IRescue once I built new enclosures, namely Bubba, Blossom, and a few others.

When I arrived, Nelson was just getting ready to leave, but he was glad to see me. We sat down and talked. He listened, agreed to everything, and said he would have the paperwork ready in a couple of days. As I left his office, I was flooded with mixed emotions: sadness at the thought of leaving Alturas, excitement for the opportunity ahead, and a little trepidation, because tomorrow I would talk to Tom.

Chapter 33

New Beginnings

I arrived back at Alturas to find Dannia and Larissa waiting for me, eager to hear what was happening. Apparently, Dannia had already explained the situation to Larissa, which was fine. I walked them through everything in detail: that Dannia would become the new director of Alturas, that Larissa would be taking on more responsibility, especially with food preparation and tours.

When they asked how Tom felt about all this, I told them the truth. He did not know exactly what was happening yet, and I was planning to talk to him in the morning. "It's probably going to be pretty ugly," I said. I knew Tom did not want me to leave the sanctuary. My tours had become incredibly popular, and they were bringing in a lot of income. And income was what Tom was all about.

That night, I did not sleep much. I tossed and turned, replaying in my head what I was going to say to Tom. In the end, I decided to keep it short and sweet, because if I tried to have a conversation with him, it was likely to spiral out of control.

The next morning, I got up, went down to the sanctuary, and made sure everything was running as it should be. Then I headed up to the restaurant to talk to Tom. I knew he would be

there around 7:30, drinking coffee, as was his custom, and
sure enough, there he was. I walked in, sat down at the table,
and said good morning. He looked up at me, and I could tell
right away he was in his typical foul mood. The conversation
began.

I told him that I had been asked by MINAE to take control
of John's sanctuary and that I had agreed. I explained that
Dannia would be taking over as director at Alturas by MINAE's
decree, Larissa would handle more of the feeding and tours, I
would be finishing out the week doing tours and training
Larissa, and that the following Monday I would be moving out
of Alturas. That last part did not go over very well.

I will not go into the details of what was said or what
happened. Suffice it to say, when the conversation ended, it
was settled. And I sincerely hoped that between then and when
I left, I would not have to speak to Tom again. I am sure Tom
felt the same way.

On my way back down to the sanctuary, I called my friend
with the box truck, the same one who had moved me to
Alturas. We made arrangements for him to come that Monday
and move me out. I got back just in time for the first tour,
found Larissa, and told her, "You're starting tour training
today."

For the rest of the week, we worked together side by side,
getting her ready. I spent much of my time in the caged area of
the sanctuary, my heart heavy. It was going to be very hard to
leave this place I had created. But my mission was to save
animals, and there were animals that needed saving up at
IRescue. Whatever was going on with Tom was just getting
worse. Alturas would continue running like a well-oiled
machine, with Dannia at the helm and Larissa and the other

staff supporting her. I had no doubt about that. So to me, the obvious and correct thing to do was to move on, to go build another animal-saving operation equal to Alturas, but on a whole new slate in the cloud forest.

By Sunday, Larissa was conducting tours on her own and doing a fair job of it. With a little more practice, I knew she would be great. That night, I finished packing all my things and had everything ready for the next morning, when the movers would arrive. They got there at 8:00 a.m. sharp. While my friend and his worker loaded the truck, I went down for one last look at what I had built, at the people who had helped me build it, at the animals we had saved. And by 10:00 a.m., I was heading down the mountain road from Alturas for the last time.

Chapter 34

Arrival in the Cloud Forest

I arrived back at Alturas to find Dannia and Larissa waiting for me, eager to hear what was happening. Apparently, Dannia had already explained the situation to Larissa, which was fine. I walked them through everything in detail: that Dannia would become the new director of Alturas, that Larissa would be taking on more responsibility, especially with food preparation and tours.

When they asked how Tom felt about all this, I told them the truth. He did not know exactly what was happening yet, and I was planning to talk to him in the morning. "It's probably going to be pretty ugly," I said. I knew Tom did not want me to leave the sanctuary. My tours had become incredibly popular, and they were bringing in a lot of income. And income was what Tom was all about.

That night, I did not sleep much. I tossed and turned, replaying in my head what I was going to say to Tom. In the end, I decided to keep it short and sweet, because if I tried to have a conversation with him, it was likely to spiral out of control.

The next morning, I got up, went down to the sanctuary, and made sure everything was running as it should be. Then I headed up to the restaurant to talk to Tom. I knew he would be there around 7:30, drinking coffee, as was his custom, and sure enough, there he was. I walked in, sat down at the table, and said good morning. He looked up at me, and I could tell right away he was in his typical foul mood. The conversation began.

I told him that I had been asked by MINAE to take control of John's sanctuary and that I had agreed. I explained that Dannia would be taking over as director at Alturas by MINAE's decree, Larissa would handle more of the feeding and tours, I would be finishing out the week doing tours and training Larissa, and that the following Monday I would be moving out of Alturas. That last part did not go over very well.

I will not go into the details of what was said or what happened. Suffice it to say, when the conversation ended, it was settled. And I sincerely hoped that between then and when I left, I would not have to speak to Tom again. I am sure Tom felt the same way.

On my way back down to the sanctuary, I called my friend with the box truck, the same one who had moved me to Alturas. We made arrangements for him to come that Monday and move me out. I got back just in time for the first tour, found Larissa, and told her, "You're starting tour training today."

For the rest of the week, we worked together side by side, getting her ready. I spent much of my time in the caged area of the sanctuary, my heart heavy. It was going to be very hard to leave this place I had created. But my mission was to save animals, and there were animals that needed saving up at IRescue. Whatever was going on with Tom was just getting worse. Alturas would continue running like a well-oiled machine, with Dannia at the helm and Larissa and the other staff supporting her. I had no doubt about that. So to me, the obvious and correct thing to do was to move on, to go build another animal-saving operation equal to Alturas, but on a whole new slate in the cloud forest.

By Sunday, Larissa was conducting tours on her own and doing a fair job of it. With a little more practice, I knew she would be great. That night, I finished packing all my things and had everything ready for the next morning, when the movers would arrive. They got there at 8:00 a.m. sharp. While my friend and his worker loaded the truck, I went down for one last look at what I had built, at the people who had helped me build it, at the animals we had saved. And by 10:00 a.m., I was heading down the mountain road from Alturas for the last time.

Chapter 35

Much to Do

That night, I slept better than I had since the initial call came in from Nelson requesting me to come here and rescue IRescue. I hopped out of bed at 5:30, full of energy, enthusiasm, and excitement, brewed up a pot of stiff black coffee, and went out behind the house to survey the situation and await the arrival of the Ticos.

Behind the house was a large concrete slab covered with a corrugated metal roof. This would be my food prep area, as well as a space where some animals could be housed. The first thing I wanted to look at was all the unused cages sitting out back. There was one large cage about 6 feet high by 10 feet long and 4 feet wide, made of metal and wire mesh. It was heavy but movable and just needed some repair on one side. It would make a good enclosure. There was also a round cage, about 3 feet in diameter and 3 feet tall on legs, that would be perfect for a single bird. Another wooden cage on legs, about 6 feet long by 4 feet wide and 3 feet high, needed to be reconstructed. This would be a project I would take on myself.

There was also a small shed where a dozen or so small bird cages were stored, the kind you would use for a canary or parakeet. These were going to be very useful in dealing with

the pericos. Against the back wall of the house was a
refrigerator, and when I opened it, I found enough assorted
fruit and vegetables in there to handle feedings for about three
more days. There were also several racks of bananas hanging
from the rafters and a good-sized outdoor sink, which was very
important.

As I rummaged around getting organized, I heard a loud
flapping of wings and a familiar honking. Out of the trees came
Harpo, honking excitedly to see me. Being greeted on my first
morning by an old friend brought a giant smile to my face. I
happily fed him some fresh papaya and banana.

As Harpo and I were reacquainting ourselves, I heard the
sound of motorcycles coming up the road. The guys were
arriving to work. The first order of business that day would be
a team meeting so I could explain my ideas while I prepared
the morning feed. We all exchanged greetings, and they told
me how happy they were that I was there. I brought out the pot
of black coffee, and we sat around the food prep table
discussing what was going to happen next.

My first question was about the four young raccoons with
the blindness problem. I had not seen them the day before and
wondered what was going on. Juan explained that they were
doing very well and were being kept in a large dog crate up in
the main house. It got a little chilly on the mountain at night,
and since they had not yet developed a proper fur coat, he was
concerned about them getting cold. Good move, Juan. He also
said that the protein diet we started four days ago seemed to
be working. Their eyes were clearing up, they were moving
around like they could see, and their fur had started to come in
thicker. That was great news.

Next, I asked about the toucan up near the main house. Juan told me the bird had been brought in by MINAE a couple of weeks earlier. It had apparently been hit by a car and was found on the side of the road, stunned and shaking. Someone picked it up and brought it to MINAE, who in turn brought it to the sanctuary. It seemed very disoriented, but upon inspection, it did not have any broken bones. They just cared for it quietly in the enclosure, and over the past two weeks, it had completely recovered. I told Juan, "We'll release that bird today, right after he's been fed."

Then I asked about the food situation, how and when food arrived for the animals. Juan explained that every Monday morning, he would go to the San Isidro farmers market and buy all the fruit and vegetables needed for the week. Then, on the way home, he would stop at a friend's house who had a tilapia pond and pick up several pounds of fresh fish. That was our protein source for the raccoons, owls, and the osprey. I told him we would need a little more fruit to last until the next trip. "No problem," he said. He would handle it and bring it tomorrow.

Next up was cage repair and new construction. With just four of us on the property, and the Ticos already tied up with regular duties, I told Juan I would talk to John to get approval to bring in a couple more workers to help with general maintenance. That way, Juan and Josué, both of whom had solid construction skills, could help me rebuild the cages and start new ones for Bubba, Blossom, and the other animals I planned to bring from Alturas.

The final issue I wanted to address in the meeting was our veterinary status. "Do we have a regular vet?" I asked. The answer was that there was a veterinarian in San Isidro they used when necessary, but he was 45 minutes away. We would have to figure out something else, maybe talk him into making bi-monthly or monthly visits.

And finally, the big parrot dome. I laid out my plan. We would move all the pericos into the small canary cages and keep them with me near the house until we could build a dedicated enclosure. Then I planned to release most of the parrots in the dome.

Now, I have previously said that releasing domesticated parrots back into the wild is a bad idea, and for good reason. They do not know how to forage. When hungry, they will fly to the nearest human settlement looking for food, and that usually ends badly. At Alturas, Tom once insisted we try releasing them, and sure enough, we had parrots flying into the hotel restaurant, landing on patrons' tables, and stealing their food. So we stopped doing it there. But this situation was different. Our nearest neighbors were miles away. I felt that if we created multiple feeding stations across the property, the parrots would stick around long enough to develop wild-foraging skills and eventually transition into a more natural life.

I was also going to take a chance on the aggressive parrot living in isolation behind the big house. My hope was that his behavior was the result of loneliness. Maybe, just maybe, if he was free to mingle, he would mellow out.

By the time the meeting ended, everyone was jacked up on strong Costa Rican coffee. Juan and Josué headed out to their daily tasks, and Taco stayed behind to help with feeding. As we prepped food together, I used my limited Spanish to get to know him better. Taco was a happy young man in his mid-20s. He had a real love for Costa Rica's animals and was eager to learn anything I could teach him. More likely, there was much more he could teach me than I could teach him. Like Josué, he was a creature of the jungle. He knew every sound, every plant. If anything was out of place, he saw it. Me? I saw a beautiful green wall. Once feeding was done, I let Taco go join the others and set off to scout locations for the new parrot feeding stations. I chose three spots, each selected for its visibility.

But before construction could begin, there was one other order of business: releasing the toucan. I headed up the hill to the enclosure near the big house. The bird had eaten all his food, so I opened the door and stepped back. It did not take long. He flew out, up into a tree next to the house, ruffled his feathers, looked around, and then took off into the distance. It was a beautiful thing. This is why I do it, for that moment, watching a healthy creature return to the wild.

Time to build the feeding stations. Each would consist of two wooden posts, five feet apart, with a five-foot-long, 18-inch-wide plank mounted across the top. Four holes would be cut into the plank to hold 12-inch food dishes. Around the platform, we would place extra posts with perches. One station would go in my yard, one across the road in the large cleared area, and one up near the big house. I grabbed the posthole digger and got to work. By mid-afternoon, the station in my yard was done, and I was making good progress on the second one when the phone rang. It was Nelson, calling from the MINAE office in San Isidro. "Are you ready to accept any new animals yet?" he asked. I told him we would need three or four more days. By then, we would have many of the dome birds released and several cages repaired. After we hung up, it was time for afternoon feeding. I headed back to the prep area behind the house and started chopping papayas, bananas, mangos, corn, everything. Right on time, Taco showed up to help distribute the food. But this time, there was one dish fewer to distribute, because there was one less resident in the sanctuary, and that alone made this a great day.

That night, John called to check in and see how things were going. We had a long conversation. I explained my plans, told him about the toucan release, and laid out my vision for the dome birds and pericos. Most importantly, I asked for approval to bring in two more workers for the next couple of weeks. He agreed. That was a game changer. With two new hires, I could pull Juan and Josué off property maintenance and get us focused on cages. I called Juan immediately and gave him the green light. He said the arrangements were already in motion, and the new guys would arrive in the morning. Everything was falling into place. Tomorrow morning, we would begin the Great Parrot Release.

Chapter 36

The Great Parrot Release

I was up early the next morning so I could watch the sun come up while enjoying my morning coffee, with Harpo, of course. Before long, I heard the motorcycles coming up the road, and I could see there was a guy on the back of Juan's motorcycle and another on Josué's. Those would be our new workers.

I gathered everyone at the food prep area for our morning meeting and laid out the plan for the day. First, I would handle the morning feeding, and then I was going to release the aggressive parrot behind the house. I did not know exactly how that was going to go. The poor bird had been suffering in isolation, and parrots are social creatures. So as long as he did not attack anybody, I was okay with letting him go free.

Once that was done, Taco and I would begin capturing and releasing the first of the birds in the dome. Juan and Josué would finish the last feeding station and then start repairing the large 6-by-10-foot cage. It should be pointed out here that one thing IRescue had in abundance was tools and materials. Under the big house was practically a hardware store, everything you could ever need to fix or build something. Tools of all types, including a torch with tanks, which Juan would use for welding the cage.

As time went on, I would discover that Juan could do it all: electrical, plumbing, welding, and he was an incredible auto mechanic. I never found anything he could not fix or build. While Juan and Josué headed off to complete the feeding station, Taco and I finished the morning feeding for the resident animals, all except for the birds in the parrot dome.

By that time, the final feeding station was completed and located not far from the cage of the isolated parrot we were going to release. I loaded the feeding station with fresh food rather than feeding the bird inside his cage. The hope was that he would fly out, see the food, and begin to feed there instead. Because the parrot was aggressive, I asked everyone to leave the area except me. My plan was simple. I would open the cage door and hope he flew out and into the nearby trees, not at me. As I approached the cage, he flung himself against the wire mesh, as usual. I moved around to the side of the cage, and he followed. Then I quickly reached around, opened the door, and waited.

It did not take long. Once the door was open, he flew out. As soon as he did, I stepped into the cage and closed the door behind me so I would be protected in case he came back for an attack. It did not go exactly as planned. Rather than flying into the nearest trees, he just kept going, off into the distance. Elated at the freedom to stretch his wings, I suppose. I could not help but wonder if we would ever see him again.

With that done, we headed down to the parrot dome. The plan for that day was to remove eight smaller Pionus parrots, about half the size of a Red-lored Amazon. We worked with two types: the white-capped Pionus and the blue-headed Pionus. Locals call them chucuyos. Of the eight in the dome, seven were white-capped, and one was a blue-headed.

All eight had been confiscated from people who had illegally domesticated them. Since they were already tame but could still fly, they had been housed in the dome. My plan was to take them out, bring them down to the food prep area, and release them near the house in hopes they would stay in the trees around the new feeding stations.

We brought four animal crates with us to the dome. When we entered with the food, as usual, the birds in the open area flew down to the feeding counter in the center of the dome, where we loaded food dishes into the sinks. This setup made it much easier, and far less stressful, to catch the chucuyos without chasing them around and stirring up panic. As we captured the birds and placed them in the crates, it became immediately obvious that they were all undernourished. Two of them had minor injuries that would prevent immediate release.

We loaded the crates in the truck and headed down to the food prep area, where we prepared to feed and then release the six healthy birds. The two injured ones were placed in individual cages, where we would treat their wounds and feed them as much as they could eat until they were healthy enough to join their free brothers.

One of the feeding stations I had built was in my yard, about 50 feet from the house and 50 feet from the tall trees behind it. The plan was to place each bird on a perch at the feeding station, one at a time. They had already been fed, but I wanted them to know the food was there. And that is exactly how it went. Each bird perched, looked around, then flew up into the big trees behind the house. Afterward, the two injured chucuyos were placed in their recovery cages and went to town on the food we gave them. It was obvious they had not been getting enough to eat in the dome, likely because only the dominant birds were getting fed. By the time that was done, Juan and Jose had completed the repair of the 6-by-10-foot cage, which was perfect, because that would be Blossom's new home. Juan asked what the next project was, and I told him it would be building a cage for Bubba.

Right behind the house was a 15-foot rise that led to a flat area filled with large trees, some mandarin, some I did not recognize. In the center of that area was a big flat spot. That is where I planned to build a 30-by-20-by-10-foot enclosure for Bubba. Juan looked at me and said, "Great idea. No problem, we'll get started right now." Music to my ears. I could not wait to get Blossom and Bubba up there with me. The last task for the day was moving the four baby raccoons out of the big house.

The plan was to relocate the young spectacled owl from the large enclosure at the bottom of the deer pen to the circular birdcage near the food prep area. Then we would move the baby raccoons into the now-vacated enclosure, about 10 by 15 by 10 feet, giving them room to exercise and develop.

I headed into the big house, where the four babies were housed in a large dog crate with their daily ration of fresh fish, fruit, and vegetables. Their eyes were nearly completely cleared up, what a beautiful sight. Three of the four were fully furred now, and the fourth was nearly there. I loaded up the crate and brought it to the food prep area. Then I grabbed a smaller crate and headed down to where the young spectacled owl was. He was beautiful and growing quickly. It would not be long before he would be ready to fly. Juan told me they had been feeding him chicken meat, which keeps him alive but is not enough to build strong bones. Owls need whole prey. They swallow it and regurgitate the fur and bones in what is called an owl pellet, but they do digest some of the calcium.

When I raised baby owls in the past, I fed them chicken necks. I would put the neck on the counter, cover it with a cloth, smash it with a hammer to crush the bones, then cut it into bite-sized pieces. Before feeding each piece, I would dip it in water with bird vitamins. That is how I raised strong, healthy owls, and that is what I would do here.

I put the young owl in the box, brought him back up, and placed him in the large round cage. I covered the cage with a tarp to reduce stress. He had been in a secluded area, and now he was in the busiest part of the sanctuary. I would uncover him after dark.

By the time Taco and I were prepping the afternoon feeding, Josué had already moved all the construction materials up to the new build site. They would be ready to start the next day. That was when I told him my plan to bring Bubba and other animals up in ten days. His reply: "The cage will be ready in eight."

Juan and the rest of the crew finished up for the day and got ready to head home. I told Taco he could leave too, and I would handle the last round of feeding. After feeding in the dome, I walked back down the hill to the house. I was delighted to see two chucuyos on the feeding station next to my house, chowing down. Another good day in paradise.

Chapter 37

The Return of Bubba and Blossom

The next two weeks flew by. So much happened in such a short time. We got all the birds out of the parrot dome that could still fly. If it could fly, I set it free. The feeding stations were working so well that I built two more. The two undernourished chucuyos were now fat, healthy, and back up in the trees with their brothers. The only downside was that by the time morning or afternoon feedings came around, they would fly down into the food prep area, landing on the table or our shoulders as we chopped fruit.

The trees outside the prep area were now full of Amazon parrots, three different types. Up the hill behind the house, Bubba's new cage was finished. The spectacled owl, now named Vincenzo, I do not know why, it just fit, had begun flapping and exercising his wings. I knew within a few days or a week, he would outgrow the round cage.

The "Gang of Four," as I had started calling the baby raccoons, were now healthy, strong, and extremely rambunctious in their lower-pen cage. They would soon be too big to contain there, but, like always, I had a plan.

We had removed ten pericos from the parrot dome, all of them flightless due to past injuries or wing clipping. These delicate little birds were often harmed when taken as pets. I housed them in parakeet cages, two to a cage. During the day, we hung the cages in the guanabana trees by the house, and at night we brought them inside and suspended them from the rafters. This routine would work until we could build a permanent perico enclosure.

Deliveries from MINAE had begun again. One morning, we received a clutch of nine baby pericos, barely out of the egg. A tree had been cut down in someone's yard, and inside was a nest. With the tree gone, the parents abandoned them, so the nestlings came to us.

We also received a new adult raccoon named Jill. She was so domesticated that all she wanted was to sit in your lap, cuddle, and eat. For now, she lived in a dog crate until I could implement my next plan.

I called my old friend Dannia, still the director at Alturas, and told her I would be coming Saturday to pick up Bubba and Blossom. We chatted a while. Things at Alturas seemed okay, but I could tell she was stressed, and I had a good idea why. Meanwhile, there was another parrot regularly using the feeding stations. I recognized him. It was the aggressive one from behind the house. He was not attacking anyone, not yet. But I kept my distance. I did not trust him. Not yet.

Taco had the feeding routine down perfectly now, both morning and afternoon. He knew exactly what to prep and how to do it, which freed me up to do other things, like repair the six-by-four wooden cage that needed new mesh. That would be where I would raise the nine baby pericos. Things were coming together nicely.

Bubba's new home was now complete. The structure was built with metal tubing and covered in chain-link fencing, strong enough to contain Bubba or any other animal. There was a raised shelf four feet off the ground that ran along the back and side, leading into a small house filled with straw, Bubba's private quarters. Later that week, John called to check in. I updated him on everything and got his approval. That was when I said, "You know what this place needs? An animal garden." I was not sure how he would take it. It would be our most expensive project so far. But I knew he had seen the garden I built at Alturas, and he had been impressed.

His response was immediate. "Do it." He told me he would send money to Juan the next day. That was huge. I walked Juan over to the area I had selected, and we took a good look. It was the large flat clearing in front of my house that I had noticed on my first day at IRescue. On the far side, nearest the jungle, there was one large tree with a two-foot-diameter trunk that stood just inside the open space. The land sloped gently down and back toward the forest, creating a natural shallow V-cut.

I explained the concept to Juan. The garden would be slightly larger than the one I built at Alturas. It would encircle the tree and the V-cut, which we would hand-dig to form a pond. A stream would be fed by our water system, and a drain would prevent overflow. Around the pond, there would be animal houses, climbing structures, and platforms. I could see the whole thing in my mind. Juan agreed. He pulled out his phone and ordered two loads of cinder block from the local hardware store, delivery scheduled for the next day. I was thrilled. Construction would probably take three weeks. By then, the Gang of Four would be ready to move out of the deer pen, and Jill would not have to live in a crate anymore.

The cinder blocks arrived Friday morning and were dropped exactly where Juan wanted them. But work would not start until Monday because the Ticos did not work weekends. Since I was planning to head to Alturas on Saturday to bring back Bubba and Blossom, I asked Taco to come in that morning and stay at the sanctuary while I was gone. He agreed.

I was up bright and early on Saturday. By the time Taco arrived, all food prep and delivery were done. All I had left was the feeding of the baby pericos. I was glad Taco was there. Feeding them had to happen every four to five hours, and I would not be back in time for the next round.

Years ago, when I first started raising baby parrots and pericos, I experimented with all kinds of complicated food, fancy formulas, and supplements. But I noticed the birds being raised by local Ticos were consistently fat and healthy, and they were not using any of that. So I started asking questions.

It turned out most were being raised on masa corn flour mixed into a paste and fed by syringe. After some painful early failures at Osa, I switched to the Tico method, and I had not lost a baby bird since. As it turned out, Taco already knew the technique. Once the babies were fed, I hit the road for Villas Alturas.

I arrived around 11:00 a.m. and found Dannia waiting for me in the staging area. We greeted each other like old friends do. She told me she was finally about to earn the law degree she had worked so hard for, and once she had it, she would be leaving Alturas. Not because she did not love the job, she did, but because the tension there had become constant. And I knew why.

She asked me for a favor. They had a raccoon named Jack who had spent his entire life confined in a dog crate. He had been overfed and had no space to move. He was so overweight and weak that he could only walk a few steps before collapsing in exhaustion. If something was not done, Jack did not have long.

I asked why they did not just put him in the garden and regulate his diet. She said the garden was full, with no more room. So I agreed to take Jack up to IRescue, knowing the new animal garden would be done in a few weeks and that he would have plenty of space there. But now, it was time. Blossom.

As I approached her cage, she was sleeping. She is mostly nocturnal. But I called her name, and immediately I heard that familiar excited grunting sound. She came charging out of her house, her little legs pumping, and climbed right into my arms, grunting happily the whole time. I gently placed her in the crate, pulled about a dozen quills out of my shirt, and put her inside the food prep kitchen to wait while I went to get the mighty Bubba.

Bubba was on the far side of the sanctuary, but he heard my voice when I called for Blossom and began going crazy in his cage. As I approached, he got even more excited. I walked into the enclosure carrying a large dog crate, and everyone around me gasped. Bubba had terrified the entire staff. No one at Alturas dared go inside his cage. But Bubba climbed into my lap, rolled over, and begged for a belly scratch. Gasps turned into exclamations of disbelief. I opened the crate. Bubba walked right in. It was like he knew. I shut the door, lifted the crate, and carried him out, chuckling as I heard people whispering, "Oh my God."

I asked one of the volunteers to help me carry Bubba back to the staging area, but he was too scared. A young woman nearby offered, and we brought Bubba back to where Dannia was waiting along with Jack and Blossom, both already in their crates. I loaded all three into the back of my vehicle, shut the hatch, and hit the road. Back to IRescue. Back to their new home. Best day ever.

Chapter 38

New Arrivals and New Beginnings

I arrived back at IRescue around 4:00 p.m. Taco had already finished the afternoon feeding and had fed the little pericos twice while I was gone, perfect. Out of appreciation for keeping the place running, I handed Taco some cash, a full day's wages, and told him he could head out. But he chose to stick around a bit longer to meet the new animals.

First order of business: get Bubba into his new enclosure. Taco helped me carry the crate up the hill into the new cage. I warned him, "You need to exit the cage and shut the door before I open this crate, otherwise it could get ugly." Taco stepped out. I opened the crate.

Bubba stepped out slowly, carefully inspecting his new home. He climbed the platform, made his way to the house we had built for him, and then returned to the edge of the platform where I stood, lowering his head for some scratching. He was happy. And I think he was relieved to be out of the sweltering coastal heat and oppressive humidity from down by the beach. I decided to give him an hour to get used to his new digs before feeding him. Then I headed back down to the food prep area to take care of Blossom.

Her crate was still on the table where I had left it. As soon as I walked up, she started to grunt, her way of communicating. I opened the crate, and she climbed right into my arms. Taco took one look and was immediately in love. I handed Blossom over to him. He looked a little nervous at first, eyeing the quills, but Blossom kept them flat against her body. She only raised them when she felt threatened, and clearly she did not feel threatened by Taco.

We had already set up a ten-by-six-foot metal cage at the back of the food prep area, under the roof to protect it from sun and rain. It had branches for climbing, a cozy house tucked into the upper corner, and a feeding station near the door, all designed with Blossom in mind. Taco gently placed her on the platform by the feeding station. She was immediately curious, already exploring. Because it was getting close to dark, her active time, she began moving about more energetically. I closed the door and figured I would feed her later, after sunset. Now for Jack. What was I going to do with Jack? There was not much to do right then except feed and water him. Tomorrow, though, we would begin his exercise and a brand-new diet, one I was sure he would not be thrilled about.

Apparently, the people who had Jack before us were feeding him cake and bread, which explained his severe obesity. He had spent his life in a dog crate, with no way to move or play. That combination had done him in. Jack did not know it yet, but his life had just changed for the better. I thanked Taco again for his help and sent him on his way. I moved to the front porch to watch the sunset, drink a couple of cold beers, and reflect on how lucky I was to be doing what I was doing.

By beer number four, it was fully dark, and I was sitting under the Milky Way in all its glory. Then I remembered: time to feed Bubba, Blossom, and Jack. Bubba got his usual mix of bananas, grapes, and watermelon, but I also gave him his favorite treat in the whole world: a hot dog. I was pretty sure he had not had one since leaving Alturas. Welcome home, buddy.

Blossom was wide awake, grunting loudly and climbing around in her cage. I gave her a dish of clean water and a big bowl of cut-up fruits and vegetables, topped with her favorite treat: ripe avocado. She quieted immediately and got to work on her dinner.

Then came Jack. Raccoons are mostly nocturnal, but he was already awake and probably hungry. I gave him a bowl of water and another with half a banana and a slice of watermelon. The look he gave me almost made me feel guilty. Everything taken care of, I returned to the porch to listen to the jungle night and say a quiet prayer of thanks before heading to bed.

The next morning, Sunday, I was up early. I was working alone and had a lot to do. Back at the food prep area, I saw that Blossom, Bubba, and Jack had cleaned their bowls, every bite gone. Jack looked at me like, "Well? Where's my breakfast?"

Blossom was curled up asleep in her little house. Bubba was clearly trying to get my attention, so I walked up to his cage and gave him a good behind-the-ears scratching. When Bubba was happy, he had this endearing habit. He would chew gently on his right front foot while being scratched. Sure enough, he was doing it right then. I headed back to begin morning feed prep. It took about an hour of chopping and mixing, and fending off food robbers the whole time.

The chucuyos were swooping in, along with a few Amazon parrots. We had also recently received a few scarlet-fronted parakeets, gitanos to the locals, bigger than pericos, smaller than chucuyos, with long tails and loud, rowdy energy. They could fly and had already been released, but they were now part of the gang, doing their best to steal food from the table. A nuisance? Sure. But honestly, it was kind of fun.

Eventually, everyone was fed except Jack, and I decided it was time for him to get a little exercise. The house had a fenced yard, four-foot chain-link. I was certain there was no way Jack could climb it or escape while I was watching. I carried the crate to the middle of the yard, opened the door, and stepped back. Nothing. Jack did not budge. Understandable. From what I knew, he might never have been outside that crate, except when it was being cleaned. He sniffed the air, peeked his head out, then retreated. So, like always, I had a plan. He was hungry. I would use that. I closed the crate door, went to the prep area, and put together a small dish of fruits and vegetables. I brought it back, showed it to Jack through the crate bars, then walked about fifteen feet away and set the bowl in the grass, fully visible from the crate. I opened the crate door again and waited. Slowly, very slowly, Jack emerged. One paw, then the other. He finally stepped fully out of the crate. That was when I got a really good look at just how fat he was. It was heartbreaking. He struggled just to walk from the crate to the food bowl.

After he finished eating, he looked up, and I could see the realization hitting him. He was outside, in the sun, in the grass, on a beautiful day. He tried to sit back on his haunches and look around, but he was too big. He toppled over. Still, he began to explore, slowly, laboriously. But it did not last long.

Within minutes, he was completely exhausted, panting from the effort of walking maybe fifty feet. Feeling sorry for him, I moved the crate over to where he had collapsed. He shuffled back inside, as quickly as his chubby legs would allow. The crate was his security. I carried him back to the food prep area, placed the crate under the roof in the shade, and gave him a big bowl of water. Which he drank and then flopped over.

I spent the rest of that beautiful Sunday taking care of the animals and thinking excitedly about the next day. Tomorrow, we would finally begin construction of the animal garden.

Chapter 39

Construction and a Fat Raccoon

The next morning, I was up extra early to feed the baby pericos, which were doing great, and to get the morning food prep underway as early as possible. About halfway through the prep, I heard vehicles coming up the road. This time, it was not just the five guys. A large truck followed behind, loaded down with bags of mortar, rebar, and everything else needed for the construction of the garden wall. Juan told me the plan was to start digging the pond inside the enclosure as soon as the truck was unloaded. "Sounds great," I told him, and added that he could have Taco for the day to help with digging. I would handle all the animal care myself.

Once I finished food prep and distribution, it was time to check on Jack. Starting that day, Jack would be placed on a mainly protein diet, combined with a daily exercise routine to help him lose weight. I pulled a couple of fresh tilapia from the fridge, filleted them, chopped them into small pieces, and placed them in a dish of water. I also included select organs and the head. I did not know if Jack had ever eaten fish before, but I knew he was hungry. I set the bowl in front of him. After a few moments of sniffing and gently feeling the contents with his front paws, he finally popped a piece of fish into his mouth and began chewing. Five minutes later, nothing was left in the bowl, and he was looking for more.

Time for exercise. I moved him out into the yard, opened the crate door, and stepped back. This time, Jack came right out with no hesitation. Once again, he began to laboriously explore the fenced yard. And once again, within just a few minutes, he was completely exhausted. I let him crawl back into the crate and moved him into the shade under the roof of the food prep area to rest.

Meanwhile, Vincenzo the spectacled owl was growing stronger every day on his diet of chicken necks and breast meat. I no longer had to hand-feed him piece by piece. He was now eating from a dish on his own. Soon, I would be able to give him whole necks and full chicken breasts to work through himself.

With a few minutes to spare, I decided to check on Bubba. It was only his second day in the new enclosure, but I wanted to see how he was doing. I entered his cage and sat down on the large boulder in the center. Bubba came right over and climbed into my lap. I scratched behind his ears, and just like always, he began chewing on his right front foot, his happy habit. I noticed immediately that he seemed less agitated and less aggressive. After thinking about it, I concluded it was probably a combination of factors. Here, he was not surrounded by the constant parade of people like at Alturas, and he was also living in a much cooler climate with lower humidity. It was simply a much more comfortable life up here.

Just then, my phone rang. It was MINAE. They asked if I could run down to the police station in Pejibaye to meet an officer and pick up three young squirrels. That was all the information they gave me. I assumed they were probably babies, so I grabbed two baby bottles, one filled with goat milk, the other with Pedialyte, which I always kept handy for emergencies. With baby animals, hydration is more critical than food in the first few hours.

The three baby squirrels consisted of a male and two females, just at the point where their eyes were beginning to open. They were of a species with beautiful markings: white, beige, brown, and black. They did not appear to be badly dehydrated. The MINAE officer said he had received the squirrels about two hours earlier, and they had been found not long before that.

The goat milk, which had been warming in the sun on my dashboard, was ready. I offered it first to the little male. He sucked it down eagerly. When I turned my attention to the females, one accepted the milk greedily, but the other not so much. She was not real happy with the artificial nipple, but eventually she too filled her belly with warm milk. Once back at the sanctuary, I set them up in their temporary homes.

I knew that getting these three little guys weaned was going to be a real handful, just like the pericos. They would require round-the-clock feedings every six hours. And baby squirrels are a test of patience. Feeding them had to be done extremely slowly and carefully, because they are prone to aspirating milk, which can be fatal if you are not cautious.

It was already time to start food prep for the afternoon feeding. By the time I finished the now ever-expanding menu and fed the ever-growing group of residents, it was quitting time for the crew working on the garden pond.

I walked over to check their progress. As expected, I was impressed. They had moved all the dirt, stacked all the rocks and mortar bags into the center of the dig, and were ready to begin shaping the pond walls and the rock stream that would flow downhill from the water source. My years in Costa Rica had taught me just how much a Tico with a shovel could get done in a day, and there were four of them on that project.

As the tired Ticos headed back down the hill, I retired to my normal evening spot with my normal cold beer, Harpo the crested guan perched on the porch railing by my side. I drank beer, gazed at the Milky Way, and fantasized about the new garden. Tomorrow would begin the stonework on both the pond and the garden wall.

Chapter 40

The Garden Opens

Over the next several weeks, Juan and his helpers finished the garden, and every inch of it was carefully inspected by Harpo. Like some feathered building inspector, he watched over the entire construction project from beginning to end, issuing the occasional series of loud honks whenever something was not to his liking. And when it was finally done, it was beautiful.

A single tree stood near the center, casting shade across half the garden. We had wrapped tin collars around the trunk. This was to prevent the raccoons from getting into the trees and possibly taking a fall. There were several houses for the raccoons, two elevated off the ground and one ground-level house designed especially with Jack in mind. The area inside the garden was real grass lawn. Two one-meter-square concrete slabs had been installed as feeding stations, one at each end, with gravel pathways connecting them. Two elevated viewing platforms rose above the garden walls, giving the raccoons a full view of their surroundings both inside and out.

The pond was around 20 feet across and 3 feet deep, with natural rock work all around its edges. A rocky stream fed into it from the front of the garden, flowing first into a bathtub-sized pool, then gently down into the main pond. I had even added tilapia to the pond, a dozen or so medium-sized ones, and floating plants danced across the surface. The garden wall varied in height, five feet at its lowest, taller where the land dropped away. It was ready, and not a moment too soon. Every cage, crate, and enclosure in the sanctuary was full. The new garden would relieve immediate pressure and give me a chance to get Juan started on new cage construction.

My plan was to introduce residents gradually. First, the two domesticated raccoons, Jill and Rocky. Next, Jack, who had come a long way in recent weeks, now roaming the yard freely with rest breaks and much slimmer than before, but still obese. After a couple of days, the Gang of Four, who had turned into four raging maniacs, fur restored, eyes bright, and in full play mode every waking minute. They had outgrown their enclosure, but they would have to wait just a few more days.

I carried over two crates containing Jill and Rocky and simply opened the doors. They came out cautiously into their new home. After a few nervous glances at each other, they both wandered toward the stream, captivated by the sight and sound of running water.

Next, I fetched Jack's crate. Jill and Rocky were still investigating the stream and pond, so I opened Jack's door. He ambled out into the shaded grass under the tree, clearly captivated both by the babbling stream and the sight of two raccoons he had seen only from a distance. Most of these raccoons had likely never interacted with their own species before.

Jack could not resist. He dragged his bulk down to the stream and lay belly-down in the water, cooling off and taking it all in. Jill and Rocky, meanwhile, had discovered the tilapia in the pond, exactly what I had hoped for. I did not think they would catch any, but the attempt would provide endless mental stimulation and physical exercise. Jack had now discovered the bathtub-sized pool and was fully immersed, feeling around the bottom with his paws, his instincts kicking in. Two days later, the garden was a hit. The three raccoons had become friendly, wrestling and playing together, enjoying their new life. It was time for the next phase: releasing the Gang of Four. Taco and I headed down to the cage in the deer enclosure with two dog crates. We captured them one by one, placing two to a crate, and carried them back up the hill. I decided to let out two at first, just to see how things went. We opened the first crate, and the two little monsters emerged cautiously, scanning their new world and then, just like the others, headed straight for the stream. Perfect. We opened the second crate. Same reaction: curiosity, then fascination with the water. Jill, Rocky, and Jack watched with simple interest. No aggression from anyone. I was relieved and proud.

Meanwhile, the young pericos had started fluttering around their cages, vigorously exercising their wings. Soon, I would open the doors and let them fly free. Their diet had matured from pure masa, to masa with papaya and banana, to just fruit with masa on the side. They had grown up strong and healthy, ready for the world.

Vincenzo, the spectacled owl, had also been released and was sticking close, perching in trees next to the house and swooping down to the feeding station I set up for him each night. I hoped he would soon disappear into the jungle.

His former cage was now home to Bubbles, a large Mealy Amazon parrot who had spent his life in a cage and suffered from a strange condition: air bubbles under his skin. Wherever a bubble formed, he lost feathers. Branches could tear him open, so he could not go in the dome or be released. Every so often, we would carefully prick a bubble with a needle, releasing the air, but it only worked temporarily.

The main parrot dome now held only non-flying birds, about a dozen. The osprey in the other dome had a band on its leg. We traced it back to Minnesota, where the bird had been banded nearly four years earlier. Somehow, it had made its way to Costa Rica, where it was struck by a car and eventually brought to us.

After feeding both domes, I was eager to check on the raccoons. It was late afternoon, and I knew they would be getting active. I walked to the wall and peeked over, not knowing what to expect. What I saw made me laugh out loud. They were all playing together. Even Jack was trying to chase two of the Gang of Four, but they were running circles around him, teasing him gleefully. Watching Jack's feeble attempts to catch the little monsters, his first real taste of freedom, was a beautiful thing.,

As twilight settled over the sanctuary, I headed back down to prep food for Blossom and Vincenzo, and to give the little squirrels their goat milk. By the time everything was done, it was dark. Time for a little stargazing, a cold beer, and some well-earned rest.

As I sat on the porch watching the Milky Way stretch across the sky, Vincenzo silently emerged from the darkness and landed in the tree in the front yard, keeping watch just like Harpo. Another magical day. And tomorrow, a new one would begin.

Chapter 41

Tommy Comes Home

The next several months were spent dialing in our procedures and expanding the number of cages and enclosures. We continued taking in new creatures, but here at IRescue, it was mostly birds. I changed the feeding schedule for the platforms from twice a day to once daily, hoping to encourage the free-flyers to forage more naturally. And it seemed to be working. We now had a resident flock that was ever-changing. Birds that had been flying around freely eventually drifted off, just as they should.

As for the new parrots that came in: If they could fly, I would keep them caged for a week to acclimate and learn where the food stations were, then let them go. If they were injured, we would rehab them as best we could and then release them if possible. And if they were unable to fly, they were transferred into the dome.

The pericos that could fly had all been released and now lived in the trees surrounding the food prep area, but they made their presence known. Every time I chopped fruit, they flew down to harass me and try to steal whatever they could.

Bubba, Blossom, and the three young squirrels were all doing great. It was just about time to open the squirrel cage and let them begin to explore the area and the yard on their own. Vincenzo and Harpo were still around, each patrolling the sanctuary on their own schedule. Harpo by day, Vincenzo by night. The garden was a complete success. I could stand there for hours watching the seven raccoons playing in the grass, wrestling, and splashing in the pond, still failing to catch a single tilapia.

One morning, months after I had first arrived at IRescue, I got a call from Dannia at Alturas. She was upset. Not long after I had left Alturas, Larissa left too. And recently, she had paid a visit to another sanctuary near the town of Quepos, a place called Kids Saving the Rainforest. That was where she found Tommy. Tommy had come into Osa as a baby with two siblings. He was partially crippled, with only about 30% use of his back legs. But despite his disability, Tommy had always been happy, enthusiastic, and never discouraged. He was one of my favorite animal personalities of all time. Now, according to Larissa, he was being kept in a small six-by-ten enclosure with a concrete floor, in the sun, with minimal shade. He was miserable. Why he had been evicted from his home at Alturas and sent to this concrete prison was unclear, but it infuriated me. I immediately got on the phone and made the calls. By the end of the day, I had MINAE's permission to bring Tommy to IRescue. I was going to rescue him first thing in the morning.

I woke up before sunrise, prepping the morning feed so that when Taco arrived, he could jump straight into distribution. That would free me up to hit the road for Quepos. I expected to get there before noon and be back by 4:00 p.m. And I was not the slightest bit worried about Taco handling things while I was gone. I arrived at Kids Saving the Rainforest right on time. A young volunteer offered to show me where Tommy was.

When we reached his cage, I had to bite my tongue. It was on the south side of a hill, fully exposed, with only a little bit of morning shade from a nearby tree. Tommy had wedged himself into the only shaded spot he could find, behind the wooden box meant to serve as a house. That was his entire life now. The volunteer girl put on a pair of welding gloves and started toward the cage to grab him. I stopped her. The Tommy I knew could be picked up and scratched. There was no way I was going to let him be manhandled by an inexperienced kid in welding gloves.

I gently moved the box aside and started talking to Tommy. He looked up. There was recognition in his eyes. But that sparkle, the one that made him Tommy, was missing. I picked him up carefully and placed him in the crate. The volunteer helped me carry him back to my vehicle, and we hit the road. I got back to IRescue late in the afternoon. Taco was waiting for me. Together, we carried Tommy's crate to the release spot we always used, the soft, shaded grass under the big tree, right next to the stream. Several raccoons had already gathered at the crate, curious about the new arrival. But no one was acting aggressive.

Inside the crate, Tommy was chittering excitedly. He wanted out. Without further delay, I opened the doors. Tommy burst out as fast as his two front legs could carry him. Once he hit the grass, he sat up on his haunches and looked around with what I swear was a raccoon's smile on his face. But what caught my attention most? That sparkle in his eyes, it was back.

He headed straight for the bathing pool and jumped in, splashing happily. I headed over to food prep to make him a special feed of watermelon and tilapia. By the time I returned to the garden, Tommy was already wrestling with Jill in the grass. The other raccoons accepted him immediately, like he had been there all along. I put his food in front of him. He dove into it like it was the best thing he had ever seen. And I just smiled and thought: Looks like Tommy's home.

That night, I sat on the porch listening to the happy chittering and splashing coming from the garden. There was a party going on over there. A celebration of second chances. And of a little raccoon finally being exactly where he belonged.

Chapter 42

Bubba's Big Leap

During the next few months, Tommy's exuberant personality came back 100 percent. Jack, once dangerously overweight, was now the size of a normal raccoon. His sagging skin had tightened up significantly, a clear sign of his transformation. Since these raccoons were now permanent residents, we began a gradual process of neutering the males, one at a time. This would not only prevent unwanted pregnancies but also help reduce fights among the males.

Everything was going so well in the garden that I decided the time had come to try something I had been contemplating for a long while: introducing Bubba to the garden. The idea was simple, to give Bubba a taste of freedom, a richer environment, and, hopefully, companionship that was not me for the first time in his life. Since arriving at the mountain, Bubba had undergone a remarkable transformation. He had mellowed out dramatically, no longer rowdy or on edge. I believed the cooler mountain climate, the quieter surroundings, and perhaps even his age, now about 14 years old, more than the natural lifespan of a wild coati, had all played a role in calming him down. Still, we had to proceed with caution. If this went sideways, it could get ugly fast, and someone could get hurt.

That morning, we fed all the animals first to avoid any food-related aggression. Then we carefully carried Bubba, inside a crate, into the garden and placed him at the usual release spot. It was a tense moment. I told Taco to leave the garden. Bubba's behavior could be unpredictable. As we waited, all the raccoons gathered curiously around the crate, checking out this strange new visitor. Bubba seemed mildly interested in them. He chittered quietly but showed none of the familiar warning signs of aggression.

Eventually, the raccoons lost interest and wandered off toward the pond, resuming their daily mission to catch the elusive tilapia. That was my cue. I opened the crate. Bubba stepped out cautiously and began exploring the garden. The Ticos, watching from over the wall with a hose ready to spray just in case a fight should break out, held their breath. Within moments, Tommy approached, sniffed Bubba, and began trailing behind him like a curious little brother. I stayed in the garden for over an hour, just to be sure.

Bubba roamed the entire space, rolling in the lush green grass, sniffing at everything, and becoming especially mesmerized by the water. Not one raccoon showed aggression, and I had no doubt that if any did, they would quickly regret it. Bubba could still hold his own. This was Bubba's first home that was not a cage, and watching him experience it brought a warmth to my heart I will never forget. He did not just tolerate the raccoons. He liked them. Before long, he was fully accepted by them. He was one of the crew. In fact, as the days passed, Bubba seemed more content than I had ever seen him. He even formed a special bond with Jill. They were inseparable. Always together. As far as Bubba was concerned, he was a raccoon now, and the garden had become the best home he ever had.

Meanwhile, Juan and Josue had been busy building more cages. We now had several new portable enclosures of different sizes. They were currently constructing a large cage for non-flying pericos, of which we had many. These birds had been living two to a cage in old canary enclosures, and we were excited to move them into something much better.

The new structure was about the size of a two-car garage. It had a tin roof for shade and rain protection, a built-in sink for cleaning dishes, an abundance of climbing branches, a misting system, two large birdbath areas, and multiple small houses for roosting. As for new arrivals, MINAE continued to bring us birds and animals.

In the past, they delivered Blind Bob, a large Mealy Amazon parrot blinded by cataracts in both eyes. He quickly became one of my favorites, a gentle, affectionate soul who loved to be held close and stroked. I kept his cage right next to the house so I could care for him personally every day.

Another time, MINAE arrived with an entire truckload of small bird cages, filled with local songbirds, finches, hummingbirds, and other tiny winged jewels. These had been confiscated from someone illegally trapping and selling them in nearby towns. Every single one of them was released. Then came a special orphan: a baby tamandua. As soon as I saw him, I named him Yoda.

I had already raised two tamanduas in my career. The first was Gomer, back when I was director at Osa Santuario de Animales, and the second was Gonzo, at Alturas Wildlife Sanctuary. The secret to success with these animals was all about the diet, and having been through it twice before, we knew exactly what to do. Yoda was still too young for his full diet, though. He would start on goat milk with small amounts of termites added in, then gradually work his way up.

And at the end of each day, after caring for all these amazing creatures, I would sit on my porch, look out into the jungle, and marvel at how much I had been blessed, always wondering what incredible things tomorrow might bring.

Chapter 43

Saved by a Forked Stick

One morning late in the third year at IRescue, I got a call from a friend who owned a hotel near the town of Uvita. He had discovered a very young collared peccary alone on his hotel grounds. It appeared to be abandoned, so he picked it up and gave me a call. He said he was about to feed it some milk. I stopped him immediately.

It was a good thing he had called, because if he had given that baby cow's milk, it would have been dead before I could even get there. As I have said before, cow's milk is for cows, and sometimes people, but it is lethal to most young wild animals. The lactose binds up their guts and kills them. Once again, the lifesaver was goat milk. I told him if he did not have any, to just give it water, and I would bring the goat milk myself.

It was already mid-morning when I hit the road for Uvita. It is a little south of Alturas near Dominicalito, so I knew I would not be back until after dark. But this was worth it, and with both Taco and Josue now fully trained and confident in animal care, I no longer needed to supervise everything.

By the time I arrived, it was mid-afternoon. My friend Frank met me outside with a small dog crate. Inside was the baby peccary. He had followed my instructions exactly and only given it water. I gave the little guy his first warm feeding of goat milk, which he sucked down eagerly.

Now a peccary may look like a pig, act like a pig, but it is not a pig. Not even close. In fact, their closest ancestor died out 50 million years ago. Still, every time I look at one, my brain still thinks pig. This one was tiny, probably weighing only two pounds. On the ride back, I already knew what I would name him: Frankie, after the man who saved him.

By the time we returned, Taco was the only one still at the sanctuary. He stuck around long enough to help me prep the biggest dog crate we had, lining it with hay while I gave Frankie another warm bottle.

From the start, Frankie was full of personality. He grew fast. He moved fast. And he acted more like a puppy than anything else. He would race back and forth across the food prep yard in full zoomie mode, hop into my lap for attention, and even bond with the sanctuary dogs like he was part of the pack.

When he finally outgrew his crate, we just let him roam free. But he always stayed close. If I stepped outside and called, "Pig! Pig! Pig!" I would hear him grunt and see him charging out of the woods at full speed, usually covered in mud from wallowing in a stream side mud hole he had discovered. In a matter of months, Frankie ballooned from that tiny two-pound orphan into a 40-pound half-grown powerhouse, and he was still growing. For now, his temperament was sweet, playful, affectionate. But I knew better than to expect it to last.

When a male peccary hits sexual maturity, things change fast. They become ill-tempered and dangerous, with razor-sharp tusks. I had seen it firsthand. Once, I had my palm sliced wide open by a bottle-crazed juvenile back at the Osa sanctuary.

In five or six more months, Frankie would be a full-grown boar. By then, he would need to move into the fenced enclosure with Mama and Junior, our two whitetail deer. That area had been left wild on purpose, giving larger animals a more natural environment to roam.

Life at the sanctuary soon fell into a smooth rhythm. Taco and Josue handled food prep and distribution on their own, which was a blessing. As much as I hated to admit it, I was starting to feel my age. The sloping terrain was taking a toll on my leg, and having two strong, reliable guys made all the difference.

A couple of months after Frankie's arrival, I got a call from MINAE. They were bringing up another peccary, this time a full-grown domesticated adult male. According to them, this peccary had lived as a companion animal for a young girl. He had even slept on the family's couch. I was skeptical. Adult males have musk glands on their backs that emit a pungent skunk-like odor. Not exactly ideal for indoor living. Still, I agreed to take him in. We would house him in the same wild enclosure planned for Frankie.

The new arrival was named Wilbur. When MINAE showed up, Wilbur was packed in a large cage at the back of their truck. He looked to be pushing 100 pounds and fully adult. It took four of us to carry the crate to the enclosure near the big house. Wilbur seemed calm enough, for now. Once we opened the door, he stepped out slowly, disappeared into the tall shrubbery, and headed down the hill. Mission accomplished, or so I thought. Since it was a Friday, that meant I would be handling the sanctuary alone over the weekend. No problem.

The next morning, I woke to moderate rain, the kind that falls steadily during the green season. I went about my normal routine. All the animals still needed to be fed, rain or not. By late morning, everything was done except the deer pen, which now included Wilbur. Because my leg was aching, I decided to use the lower gate and feed station. The upper gate would have required climbing the hill, while the lower trail was shorter and relatively flat, about 100 yards long once through the gate, hugging the slope. I carried the food in one hand and a seven-foot-long forked walking stick in the other, a heavy staff with twin prongs at the end. It was just for balance on the muddy slope. Or so I thought.

The trail was only about 12 inches wide, slick with rain that was still coming lightly, and perched along a 45-degree incline that dropped to the creek below. A slip could mean a painful tumble. I moved carefully along the trail, scanning the hillside for any sign of Wilbur. Nothing. I reached the feeding station, unloaded the food into the trough, and gave my usual whistle to call the deer. Suddenly, from up the hill, I heard deep grunting. Then I saw the shrubbery begin to shake. Wilbur was coming. Fast. At first, I thought: He is hungry. He smells the food. But within seconds, I knew better.

His fur was bristled, a sure sign of aggression. The grunting turned to snarling, and he was charging straight at me. In a desperate move, I grabbed a half-papaya from the trough and tossed it toward him. Maybe he would go for it. He did not even blink. He thundered past the fruit, eyes locked on me, full tilt. I had no choice. I braced myself and began backing down the slippery, narrow trail, keeping the forked stick in front of me like a shield. Wilbur hit it immediately, gnawing and thrashing, trying to get past it. I used every ounce of strength I had to keep him back, each footstep a careful test of the trail behind me. It was a nightmare. If I slipped, I would be on the ground, and Wilbur would be on top of me. And it was about 100 yards to the gate.

Step by step, inch by inch, I fought my way backward through the mud. The rain was coming down. The footing was treacherous. Wilbur never let up. He attacked the stick constantly, snarling, lunging, pure fury. Minutes stretched into what felt like hours. Finally, I felt concrete under my foot, the slab at the base of the gate. With one final shove, I forced Wilbur back just long enough to unlatch the gate, slip through, and slam it shut. He was on it immediately, gnawing the metal, still frenzied. I collapsed in the mud, heart pounding, rain pouring down. I was shaking, not from fear, well, maybe a little, but from adrenaline. And I was thanking God for that forked stick, the very one I almost did not bring.

Chapter 44

Reflection in the Cloud Forest

The next morning, Sunday, I was once again alone at the sanctuary. That was nothing new. I could handle the daily workload just fine, but after what happened with Wilbur the day before, I would be lying if I said I was not a little uneasy about going into the deer pen again. This time, I decided to enter through the upper gate. It was only about ten feet from the feeding station, which gave me a quick escape route if Wilbur decided to pick up where he left off.

When I reached the gate, all three animals, Wilbur and the two deer, were waiting near the trough, clearly expecting breakfast. The big question was: How do I get in without being mauled? Wilbur was right at the fence, grunting, sizing me up, and I could not get a solid read on his mood. He was not showing aggression, but he was not exactly wagging his tail either. I was not about to roll the dice and stroll in. So, I pulled a papaya out of the basket and let him sniff it through the fence. He was interested. Very interested. So I lobbed the papaya over the fence and watched it tumble down the hill, and sure enough, Wilbur gave chase.

As soon as he disappeared into the brush, I opened the gate, darted inside, dumped the feed into the troughs, and got out fast. Success. But I had no illusions. We were not going to be able to fool him with the same trick every time.

As the months passed, I found myself well into my third year at IRescue. Whatever had kept John in Colombia had kept him far longer than expected, but he had recently contacted me and said he would be returning soon. In the meantime, the animals at the sanctuary were thriving. Bubba was living his best life in the raccoon garden. He loved his freedom, his pond, and most of all, his new friends. The raccoons had completely accepted him as one of their own. Blossom was doing beautifully. Every night I would visit her, and she would greet me with affection and curiosity, always happy to see me.

The feeding stations for the parrot flock were working exactly as I had hoped. New birds would arrive, mingle, and sometimes drift off to join wild flocks. It was the kind of dynamic ecosystem we had dreamed of. The flightless pericos were thriving in their new enclosure, while those who could fly spent their days zipping around the house and yard. Most mornings, I would step outside and be immediately mobbed by eight or ten little green flying jewels, landing on me and demanding breakfast. Vincenzo was still our nighttime guardian. Like clockwork, just after sunset, I would place some chicken on the table, and he would swoop silently out of the dark, snatch it mid-flight, and vanish back into the trees.

Harpo was still running the day shift. When he was not perched somewhere acting like a feathered supervisor, he was patrolling the sanctuary like he owned the place, making sure no women snuck in while he was not looking. Frankie, now a full-grown peccary, somehow maintained his sweet and gentle nature, a rare trait in an adult male. Because of that, we let him roam freely around the sanctuary grounds. He had earned it.

Behind the small house, the trees were alive with squirrels, some little black ones, along with three of the multicolored kind. And now, during food prep, I was not just fending off Chucuyos, Amazon parrots, and pericos, I also had to deal with food-thieving squirrels leaping onto the counter like fuzzy little pirates. Taco and Josue had become as good at animal care as anyone I had ever worked with. They knew the diet, routine, and needs of every single animal in the sanctuary. I trusted them completely.

One night, I sat on the porch, Vincenzo perched silently in the tree, Blossom curled up in my lap. The stars overhead were brilliant, the jungle alive with sound. And I thought back. I remembered how it all began.

I was a vendor on Dominical Beach, the only vendor for an entire year. Now, the beach was crowded with so many vendors, there was not room for a single one more.

While working that beach, I sent more than 30 rescued puppies back to the States, each one adopted into a new life.

I founded D.A.W.G., which continues to spay, neuter, and save domestic animals across southern Costa Rica.

I built a 4,200-square-foot house in the jungle, complete with seven bedrooms and four bathrooms.

I searched for, and found, gold on the Osa Peninsula.

I created Osa Santuario de Animales, the first wildlife sanctuary in the southern zone. It still operates to this day, under new management, continuing to save wild lives.

I created Alturas Wildlife Sanctuary, which also continues to excel, now considered Costa Rica's premier wildlife sanctuary.

And I had resurrected IRescue, breathing new life into a place that had been on the brink of collapse. Now it was thriving, full of life, color, and purpose.

But as I sat there, with a cold beer in one hand and the night jungle all around me, I came to a realization: I could not do it forever. I was fifty when this all began. And now, with seventy staring me in the face, I knew it was time to think about what came next. I was proud, deeply proud, of what I had done. I knew that after me, the sanctuaries I had built would continue to save animals. The systems, the teams, the legacies were in place. But it was bittersweet. Because I loved this life.

I polished off the last of my beer, scooped Blossom gently in my arms, carried her to her cage, and began pulling a couple dozen quills out of my shirt. I stroked her once more, said good night, and headed inside. Because tomorrow... there would be another animal or another bird that needed help.

And I would be ready.

Epilogue

I left Costa Rica in the spring of 2019, driven by personal and health reasons. The narrative you have just read is completely true, but by no means complete. In its current form, it is little more than a bare-bones recounting of my years in the jungle. A simple outline. A threadbare roadmap. To fully capture the depth of what happened, to bring life to all the characters, both human and animal, who crossed my path, would take several books.

I could easily fill an entire volume with just the stories from the banana bread table, the laughter, the strangers, the wild conversations, the unexpected connections. I could write a book for each sanctuary, Osa, Alturas, and IRescue, each with its own cast of unforgettable personalities, moments of crisis, triumph, heartbreak, and growth that I could not fit into this narrative.

There are so many stories left to tell.

The only question is...

Will I?

About the Author

Mike Graeber spent over twenty years living and working in Costa Rica, where much of his time was dedicated to wildlife rescue and sanctuary operations.

With no formal training in biology, veterinary science, or wildlife management, he learned through direct experience in one of the most unpredictable environments on Earth.

Working with monkeys, sloths, and exotic birds, he faced daily situations where instinct, timing, and courage were often the only things standing between success and failure.

These are real experiences, told by someone who lived them — offering a rare, unfiltered look into the world of wildlife rescue.

www.ingramcontent.com/pod-product-compliance
Lightning Source LLC
Chambersburg PA
CBHW031122130726
47988CB00006B/2191